Writing with Sources

A Guide for Students

Writing with Sources

A Guide for Students

Third Edition

Gordon Harvey

Hackett Publishing Company, Inc.
Indianapolis/Cambridge

Acknowledgments
Thanks are due again to the helpful advisors and readers of earlier editions; to Deborah and Laura at Hackett, for their patience; and to the valiant editors of the major publication manuals and guides, as they try to keep up with the flux of source kinds and citation styles, and from whom I have gratefully borrowed the occasional example in the appendix.

For further information, please address
       Hackett Publishing Company, Inc.
       P.O. Box 44937
       Indianapolis, Indiana 46244-0937

       www.hackettpublishing.com

Cover design by Deborah Wilkes
Composition by William Hartman

Library of Congress Cataloging-in-Publication Data

Names: Harvey, Gordon, 1953– author.
Title: Writing with sources : a guide for students / Gordon Harvey.
Description: Third Edition. | Indianpolis : Hackett Publishing
    Company, Inc., [2017] | Includes bibliographical references.
Identifiers: LCCN 2016044099 | ISBN 9781624665547 (pbk.) |
    ISBN 9781624665554 (cloth)
Subjects: LCSH: English language—Rhetoric. | Research—
    Methodology. | Report writing.
Classification: LCC PE1478 .H37 2017 | DDC 808/.042—dc23
LC record available at https://lccn.loc.gov/2016044099

Contents

Check for updates and other materials at
www.hackettpublishing.com/wws3-support

TOPIC BOXES

Preface

Knowledge never stands alone. It builds upon and plays against the knowledge of previous knowers and reporters, whom scholars call *sources*. These are not, in a paper, the source of your argument (you are), but rather of information and ideas that help you discover, support, and articulate that argument.

At a university, the questions that most engage you—to which you have been drawn by the writing and speaking of others; i.e., by sources—are not the sort that can be answered quickly or resolved to a certainty. You can only suggest the probable truth of your answer by making a strong case that wins the assent of others. Making a strong case to scholarly others—to an audience of students and teachers of a subject who wish to understand it as fully and firmly as possible—involves not only drawing on sources, but taking special care in their use and acknowledgment.

This booklet describes the expectations and techniques for taking care that are common across disciplines. It does not discuss how to search for sources, a topic best pursued in the context of particular courses and disciplines. Knowing how sources are used and acknowledged, however, can make it easier to know what you're searching *for*. It can also keep you from taking valuable time away from the creative process of writing. And it can keep you from slipping into plagiarism—an increased danger in the era of cut-and-paste, when thousands of sources are instantly available.

But the challenge of writing with sources remains what it always has been. It's the challenge of finding your own voice in the midst of many other voices; of discovering in the constant presence of teachers something that you yourself have to teach;

of going beyond the many sources that surround and inform you to become a source yourself.

The principles outlined here apply to digital and print sources alike. Even if you believe that you already understand when and how to document sources, you should compare your understanding with what follows. Above all, because some conventions vary between disciplines, don't hesitate to ask your instructor about situations that are unclear to you.

Preface to Third Edition

The experience of writing with sources continues to change, as the kinds of stored material and ways of consulting that material multiply. The experience has in some ways become easier, in the age of digital connectedness, and in some ways harder. Social life increasingly consists in acts of writing and sharing sources casually, often on the same screen and at the same time as one is writing a paper that requires using sources carefully!

The conditions of our digital lives—the replacement of the library by the laptop; the flood of new information and opinion (and the daunting amount of old) that is so easily accessible; the pressure on a student's time of maintaining an online identity and relationships, and on the student's psyche of increasing competition for grades and jobs—makes more challenging the act of using sources responsibly, and also more vital.

The good news is that, although the challenges of taking care have increased, the principles and guidelines for doing so remain the same. This edition of *Writing with Sources* makes more reference to digital media but preserves the structure and content of earlier editions. It sharpens the summaries at the start of chapters, breaks up some of the longer blocks of text, and uses a more spacious, two-color type face. Finally, the book is now linked to a web page (www.hackettpublishing.com /wws3-support) that provides, among other resources for writers, updates on citation formats in the different styles.

1

The Role of Sources

What *is* a source? Almost any record of experience *can* be one, if it can be consulted by others: a painting or video clip or letter, a radio broadcast or blog entry, a review from a defunct magazine or statistics from a weather balloon. It becomes a live source, however, only when it becomes a source *of* something for somebody, when it plays a particular role in a particular scholar's work.

Writing with sources doesn't mean dropping them impressively into your paper, but engaging with them in a way that puts them to work for you. It means—and this is the central point of the book—taking charge. This chapter gives some basic options for doing this—for employing a source as information, opinion, concept, and comparison—by defining your stance toward its implications. The chapter then suggests that sources will work for you most effectively if they are reliable and you can be counted upon to cite them reliably, so your reader can proceed through your argument with trust. Acknowledging your sources fairly, therefore, boosts both your self-respect and your persuasiveness.

1.1 Sources of What?

A source usually provides a paper with one of two things: (1) it provides *factual data* to interpret and use as evidence, or (2) it provides *ideas about* data, to build upon or dissent from. A distinction is sometimes made on this basis between "primary" and "secondary" sources (see Box A). More specifically, a source of factual data usually provides one of the following:

- *exact text* of a written, spoken, or visual composition (such as that provided in a published edition or on an audio or video recording);

- *statistics or measurements* (such as those tabulated or graphed in a research article);

- a *summary record* of an experience (such as that given in an ethnographic report or eyewitness testimony);

- *information* (such as that assembled in a biography or a textbook).

When a source provides a paper with ideas, it is often providing one of the following:

- a particular *claim* made by another writer about the topic you are addressing, along with the reasoning that supports the claim; or

- a general *concept*—a term, theory, or approach—that has appeared in discussion of other topics and that you apply to your own.

Either facts or ideas, finally, may be brought into a paper in the role of a *comparative case,* which illuminates the main case under consideration by similarity or contrast.

But to make use of a source in any of these ways, a writer must define a stance toward it. The three basic stances you can take toward a source are *yes, no,* and *sort of.* You can affirm or accept it, and say to it, *"Yes, and so. . . ."* You can reject or disagree, and say to it, *"No, rather. . . ."* Or you can qualify or modify the source, and say to it, *"Yes, but . . . ," "Yes, except . . . ,"* or *"Yes, if. . . ."*

Your stance toward a source of factual data will often be one of acceptance, although you may call into question the completeness or accuracy of provided facts; your stance toward sources of ideas will vary. All scholars, in making their contribution to the larger understanding of a subject, accept and build on the work of others, but they often discover where their contribution lies through reasoned disagreement with and qualification of that work.

A student writer, Jeff, having done much reading for a term paper on the Civil War, has sketched out the following proposal to organize his thoughts. *Italicized* words suggest what a source will be a source of; **CAPITALIZED** words suggest the stance that Jeff will take toward it:

> The ***claim*** of many historians that the North won the war with greater manpower and resources is true, **BUT** such a large event has many contributing causes. Linn and others have ***proposed*** that Lincoln's leadership was crucial. I will **SUPPORT** this ***view*** **BUT** argue that a particularly influential and underestimated aspect of that leadership was his skill at crafting memorable speeches on key occasions to give immediacy to abstract ideals.

As the italicized words indicate, some of the articles that Jeff has read will provide this argument with claims (*proposals, views*) about why the North won. Toward these claims, as the capitalized words suggest, Jeff's stance in his paper will be "*Yes, but.*" He won't try, wisely, to refute outright a scholarly consensus about material resources, but rather will qualify the importance claimed for them. Likewise, Jeff will modify the claims made for the importance of Lincoln's leadership by focusing on a specific aspect that he thinks deserves more notice.

These moves of qualifying and modifying will provide the motive for Jeff's paper. In the rest of his proposal, again, *italicized* words indicate what his sources will be sources of, and **CAPITALIZED** words indicate the stance Jeff will take toward them:

I first **ACKNOWLEDGE** the importance of the North's material resources in the outcome of the war, citing statistical **data. BUT** I then give **examples** of cases where inspiring leadership influenced military outcomes in the face of resources. Referring especially to the **example** of Churchill's galvanizing speeches in WWII, I invoke Simmons's **USEFUL** *notion* of "rhetorical turning points." I **compare** Lincoln's situation to Churchill's and note the *fact* that he **TOO** at key points in a war came up with striking and stirring phrases to unify his audience.

I then analyze the **details** of several Lincoln speeches to show how he creates "moral vividness" (in the linguist Denby's **APT** *term*) by finding the right metaphors for the occasion. I trace the effect of his words by analyzing the **report** of the speeches in subsequent newspaper accounts. I **contrast** these speeches with speeches given by the Southern leader Jefferson Davis that, in a similar situation, do **NOT** have the same effect.

To **REFUTE** a possible objection to my argument, I address the **claim** implied in several popular accounts of Lincoln's life that his skill at speaking was not crafted responding to a particular situation but a natural product of his simple and direct personality. I **compare** the **texts** of early speeches and speeches in draft form to the **QUITE DIFFERENT** speeches Lincoln later gave, to show that he worked deliberately to create his effects. I **DRAW UPON** *evidence* of his letters and conversations to show that he was aware of the historic work that his speeches had to do.

Some of the works that Jeff has read will provide his paper with factual data, as indicated by the words *report, details, texts, evidence,* and *fact.* They will document the fact that Lincoln did give speeches at key junctures, what exactly Lincoln said and wrote, what concerns were on his mind at the time, and what impact the speeches had. Accepting the accuracy of these sources, Jeff's stance will be *"Yes, and so."* He will say *"Yes, and so"* also to the applicability of certain general concepts: Simmons's *useful notion* and Denby's *apt term.* And finally, some of Jeff's sources will provide comparative cases. He accepts the fundamental comparability of Churchill's situation to Lincoln's, saying *"Yes, and so."* He denies the comparability of Davis's speeches to Lincoln's (*"No, rather"*) and of Lincoln's drafts with his delivered speeches; and he will use the latter contrast to refute the claim that Lincoln's speeches emerged naturally from a homespun character.[1]

These source roles are common in scholarly writing of all kinds and to all kinds of student assignments. Shorter assignments may invite you to work with only one of these source roles. You may be asked to analyze a piece of complex textual data (e.g., argument, poem, novel, film), to agree or disagree with a given claim, to apply a general theory to a particular case, or to compare two works or how two theories apply to a case.

Longer assignments, for which you may be required to define your own issue and find your own sources, expect you to use those sources in whatever ways are required to make a

---

1. Writing out this kind of source plan can be useful. It's just a proposal, but writing it forces Jeff to bring his sources into a purposeful order, based on his own thinking, and allows him to move forward. His plan may turn out to be too ambitious: he may find he lacks enough information to attribute a precise impact to speeches. Rather than taking on directly the large issue of what won the war, he may end up focusing (as good papers often do) on the workings of one or two primary documents—speeches and letters—in the *context* of the large issue. But because he has sketched a plan in advance, the difficulties will become apparent early—to Jeff himself or to others with whom he shares his plan (see section 3.4 #9).

persuasive case for your way of looking at the material. Since you will be relatively new to the field in question and can't possibly know all the scholarship, that way of looking isn't expected to be completely new, but it is expected that you'll put sources together in your own way, or use them to say something of your own, not just repeat them.

[A] "PRIMARY" AND "SECONDARY" SOURCES

Sources called "primary" generally appear in papers as sources of uninterpreted factual data, and those called "secondary" as sources of interpretive ideas; but keep in mind two cautions.

First, although a source may be categorized as primary or secondary as it sits on a shelf or in a database, it can often be used as primary in one situation and secondary in another. An article that offers a new interpretation of *Hamlet* would be a secondary source if you were writing a paper on the meaning of that play; if you were writing about a new style in writing literary criticism, the same article would be primary data for you to analyze and use as evidence.

Second, the use of the terms *primary* and *secondary* differs across disciplines. Usage in the humanities and fields primarily studying texts follows the basic distinction above. In the empirical sciences, however, *primary sources* are research articles that provide new data but also offer an interpretation of that data. A *secondary source* is an article that summarizes and reviews data from previous research articles, and may or may not offer new interpretations. Because interpretations change rapidly as more data is collected, however, research articles in the sciences do tend to be cited by other papers more often for their results than for their interpretations.

1.2 Citing Reliable Sources

The persuasiveness of a scholarly paper depends on a persuasive deployment of sources in clear roles, but it also depends on the reliability of the sources being deployed. Suppose Jeff's sources for his paper on Lincoln had turned out to be these:

- for the prevailing view of what won the war: a Confederate War re-enactors website and a student report posted on a personal website;

- for the facts of Lincoln's life and speaking occasions: websites of the Honest Abe Society, a Pennsylvania Battlefield Tours website, and a Wikipedia article;

- for early drafts of Lincoln's speeches: a typed handout from Jeff's high school debate class;

- for Davis's speeches: Internet excerpts from an 1880 edition edited by Davis's cousin;

- for his account of Churchill and historical turning points: a summary of Simmons's book in *Time* magazine, a page called "Speaking to Win" on leadership .com, and a year-old blog.

These sources, neither written nor checked by authorities in the field, out-of-date in some cases and impossible to consult in other cases, are likely to be inaccurate or at best incomplete in their accounts. And they will be variously influenced by regional bias, by the profit motive, and by a need to be brief and breezy for a popular audience.

A scholarly reader of Jeff's argument would feel let down. Scholarly readers are students or teachers of a subject who seek to understand it and to base their understanding on strong demonstrations. They expect scholarly writers, even writers relatively new to the topic, to be similarly serious seekers. They expect them at least to use the time and the resources at their disposal *as* scholars to make the strongest case they can. This means taking the time to find and use sources that can be trusted to provide full, accurate, and unbiased material and thus provide a stable ground for demonstration. The paper imagined above suggests no serious effort in this regard, but only a quick Google search.

It isn't always easy to know, when you're new to a scholarly field, which sources are serious. But learning to assess the source of one's information, ideas, and attitudes is part of an education in critical thinking. This assessing habit has become all the more useful now that so much information, and so many ideas and implicit attitudes, are being assembled, packaged, and repackaged on the Internet.

You can take your initial cue, in assessing sources, from the kinds of sources that are assigned as readings in your classes:

- standard, up-to-date editions of texts (the editions used in current articles in the field, whose bibliographies can also be used to determine which books and articles are currently important);

- scholarly articles—not from popular magazines but from journals whose contents have been assessed by scholars in the field, which therefore reflect ideas that the field takes seriously and that handle sources carefully;

- compilations of data—historical, biographical, and statistical—that reflect the current state of knowledge in a field.

Sources such as these, which can be trusted to provide accurately the information and ideas they offer to provide, are readily available to members of a scholarly community (see Box B). And their notes and references are better starting points for finding other sources than a Google search.

It's not the case that anything written for a popular audience, rather than an academic one, should be distrusted. Because such works are often both lively *and* reliable, they do appear on college syllabi. Nor is it always unacceptable, when working on a paper, to see what a general web search turns up. Even professors do this—Google a topic, for example, and visit Wikipedia—as a first pass or to get basic or tangential information.

Their actual papers, however, do not depend on the result of casual searches, and neither should you. Doing so increases your risk not only of plagiarizing (see Chapter 3), but also of making factual errors. A general Google search (as opposed to one in Google Scholar, say) brings before you as many unreliable sources as reliable ones and puts you in the position of having to tell them apart in short order, which you may not yet know enough about the field to do. The fact that a website gets many hits or has multiple links is no guarantee that its information is reliable.

[B] ASSESSING INTERNET SOURCES

The best way to locate reliable sources is to go through a website of a scholarly library that gives you access to databases, indices, texts of abstracts and journals, collections of statistics, maps, paintings and photographs, and many other resources, often organized by field. Electronic sources available through these library portals are chosen for scholarly authority and reliability. Instructions linked to the library portal page show you how to first find the sources best suited for your search and then how to best search them for the information you want.

Generally, use websites and other non-journal and nonbook materials from the Internet only to supplement other sources. When you do use them,

- Give priority to those that list their sources (so you can verify the information) or at least list an advisory board of professionals who vet the material.

- If the site doesn't list its sources but still seems serious (i.e., shows no breeziness, carelessness, or bias, and isn't a commercial [*.com*] site), check out the author's professional position and what else he or she has written, and whether the site has a respectable institutional base or is an outgrowth of a long-standing professional organization. You can also directly e-mail the author about the status of a particular piece of information—or post a query.

- Don't use as a source a site that gives no author or supervisory editor.

- When the text on a site is subject to change or erasure, and thus may not be consultable by other readers, try to find a more stable source for the information. If you must use it, either print out the text or have the author send it to you as a personal communication—which you can then cite as such and attach to your paper as an appendix.

If you include non-journal Internet sources in your paper and you have, or think your reader may have, concerns about their reliability or verifiability, include an explanatory note (see section 2.5).

1.3 Citing Sources Reliably

However reliable your sources may be, your reader must be able to *see* that they're reliable and trust that you are acknowledging them reliably—that you are reliably making clear what comes from you and what comes from your sources. You show this by citing, making a notation in your paper that refers to publication information you provide elsewhere (common methods are described in Chapter 4).

But what constitutes reliability in citing? When should you cite—and why? You should cite on the following occasions:

(a) *Whenever you use factual material—e.g., data, information, testimony, or a report—that you found in a source.* You need to make clear to your readers *who* gathered the information and *where* to find its original form. Even if these matters are common knowledge in the field, if *your* knowledge of them isn't firsthand, your readers need to know where your version of the facts came from.

(b) *Whenever you use ideas—e.g., claims, interpretations, conclusions, or lines of reasoning—arrived at by another person,* so your readers know that you are summarizing thoughts formulated by someone else, whose authority your citation invokes, and whose formulations readers can consult and check against your summary.

(c) *Whenever you use a special concept, term, or theory that you found in a source.*

(d) *Whenever you make use of a source passage's distinctive structure, organizing strategy, or method,* such as the way an argument is divided into distinct parts, sections, or kinds; the way a distinction is made between two aspects of a problem; or a new procedure for studying some phenomenon (in a text, in the laboratory, or in the field) that was developed by a particular person or group. Citing tells your readers that the strategy or method isn't yours and allows them to consult its original context.

(e) *Whenever you quote verbatim.* When you cite a passage of two or more words in a row, or even a single word (a characterization or label, for example) that is distinctive or striking. Your readers need to be able to verify the accuracy and context of your quotation, and to credit the author of the source for crafting the exact formulation. Words you use verbatim from a source must be put in quotation marks, even if you use only two or three words; it's not enough simply to cite. (If you go on to use the quoted word or phrase repeatedly in your paper, as part of your analytic vocabulary, you don't need to cite it each subsequent time; however, you do need to attribute the terms at the outset.)

You should cite for all of these occasions, even in situations that may seem to you nonstandard. The rules apply, that is, to

- **all uses of sources:** including summaries and paraphrases, even where the source provides only "background" information to your argument (such as historical context or a survey of previous work done);

- **all types of assignments:** including problem sets, computer programs, lab and other reports, collaborative projects, and take-home exams (the fact that your instructor may recognize your use of a course text doesn't change the need to acknowledge it);

- **all types of sources and media:** including numbers, images, graphs and charts, oral communications, films and videos; media including Internet and databases, class sourcebooks and class texts, and lectures.[2]

Finally, although you aren't required to mention the help you have received informally, acknowledging such help is a generous and honest gesture and a good habit to develop (see Box C).

1.4 Why Cite?

Why cite so scrupulously? The consequences of discovered plagiarism (see section 3.1) are to be avoided, obviously, but doesn't frequent citation weaken a paper by making you seem less thoughtful and too dependent on others? Yes, if you find yourself citing sources for almost everything in your paper or even for entire paragraphs, you have a problem. You may be citing "common knowledge" (see Box D) or citing inefficiently (see Box O); or, more likely, you're giving too much rehash of

---

2. A lecture is a carefully constructed presentation by an authority in the field, and may itself draw on other authorities; thus, you should cite if you use a distinctive idea, phrase, or piece of information from a lecture. Some instructors may want you to regard their lectures, given for the purposes of their class only, as common knowledge not to be cited. Ask about this before incorporating lecture material.

[C] ACKNOWLEDGING UNCITED SOURCES

Whenever you write a paper of more than a few pages, you draw on many influences: not only sources you can cite as sources of something definite, but also less immediate, less definite sources, such as the lessons of former teachers, conversations or e-mails with friends, class discussions, or an inspiring book you read over the summer. When you have benefited substantially from ideas in sources like these that won't appear in your list of references, you should acknowledge them in a footnote or endnote (see section 2.5). Doing so shows you to be both generous and intellectually self-aware.

Remember, however, that your sources may themselves be using phrases and ideas from their reading or lectures. If you write a paper that depends *heavily* on an idea you heard in conversation with someone, you should check with that person about the source of the idea. Also be aware that no instructor will appreciate your incorporating his or her ideas from conversation verbatim into your paper, but will rather expect you to express the ideas in your own way and to develop them.

other people's ideas and need to generate more of your own—you need to step beyond your sources. But once you have a case to make, careful citing is at once a service, a moral obligation, and an argumentative advantage.

Your citation says several things to your readers. For one, it says, *"Here is where I found this idea, these words, or this information. Here you can verify the summary of the idea I am giving you or find the full context for the words I have paraphrased or quoted—in case you wish to check them or pursue the matter yourself."* Your citation allows your readers to find in a source what you have found and to make use of it themselves. Such readers are particularly grateful to have it made clear, moreover, exactly what in your paper comes from the source and what comes from you.

Your citation also says, *"This person deserves the credit for gathering these materials together or for coming up with these thoughts or words; I hereby acknowledge my indebtedness."* Saying this is only fair to the author in question. Life is short, and he or she has spent many precious hours and days working out the ideas and words that you are casually perusing, assuming that he or she would be fairly credited for them. If you don't credit the author for this work, you implicitly credit yourself for it. If you credit vaguely or sloppily, you create confusion in the minds of others as to what the scholar has accomplished, probably in the process making the accomplishment seem less than it is.

Citing is only fair, also, to the community of students and teachers of which you are a part. It is only fair to other students in your class who fairly acknowledge any help they get from sources. It is only fair to your instructors, who agree to take your ideas seriously—even when they are uninformed and fragmentary—so long as you take the scholarly process seriously by taking yourself seriously as a thinker and as a potential source for other thinkers. When you pretend to have thought or written something that you haven't, you aren't honoring the bargain, and you are treating the process as a game.

Being helpful and fair in your citing also makes your argument stronger. When you analyze data or text from a source, your citation says, *"This scholar has collected the material I'm working with (as you can verify); it's a reliable basis for my conclusions."* When you support or build on a source's idea, it says, *"These learned scholars have found this to be so; it's not just my idiosyncratic opinion or blithe assumption."* When you challenge an idea, it says, *"This learned scholar has this view, as you can verify for yourself: I am not taking on a fool, or creating a straw man."* Citing not only gets you credit for having read these scholars; it also makes your own contribution stand out against the contributions of others—others whose company elevates you.

Reliable citing strengthens your paper, finally, by manifesting intellectual character. It establishes you as not just honest but also helpful, open and generous, serious, careful, and confident enough in your own thinking and reading, and in the intellectual process, to give credit where it is due—to acknowledge other views. Intermittent, casual, sloppy, or vague citing raises suspicion and makes your readers skeptical; ready and consistent citing puts your readers in a generous state of mind, willing to notice and give *you* full credit for the thinking you have done.

[D] "COMMON KNOWLEDGE"

Unless you are closely studying it, you don't need to cite a phrase like "all the world's a stage" or "life, liberty, and the pursuit of happiness." These are common locutions, known to all educated readers. Nor do you need to cite information that is either familiar to educated readers or easily available in many general sources (such as encyclopedias, dictionaries, and basic textbooks). The date of Lincoln's Gettysburg Address, the distance to Saturn, the structure of the American Congress, the date of birth of the discoverer of DNA, the fact that Sigmund Freud developed such ideas as the unconscious and the Oedipus complex—such information, in its basic form, is widely accepted and not based on a particular interpretation or point of view; it counts as common knowledge. In the paper excerpted on p. 23, Jennie doesn't need to cite her passing references to the notion of "oral fixation" (line 6) or the fact that gentlemen used to have an after-dinner cigar separate from the ladies (lines 40–41).

The line between common and uncommon knowledge isn't always clear, but it is your responsibility to take care that an assumption of common knowledge doesn't lead you into plagiarism. If Jennie had gone on to say that the after-dinner cigar ritual occurred even in matriarchal societies—an unfamiliar idea brought to light by the work of certain scholars—she would have needed to cite a source, both to show that the idea has a solid basis and to credit those scholars. If Jennie's argument had mentioned particular aspects of Freud's fixation theory, details that aren't familiar to most readers, she would have needed to cite Freud (or the source for her account of his theory). She would have needed to cite in this paper written for her ethics class, even though the details of Freud's theory *had* been common knowledge in the psychology seminar she took the previous semester. Ideas that are common knowledge in one academic field are often not in other fields. When in doubt on this score, ask—or cite anyway, to be safe.

Note, finally, that when you draw a *great deal* of information from any single source, you should cite that source even if the information is common knowledge, since the source (and its particular way of organizing the information) has made a significant contribution to your paper.

2

Integrating Sources

Having used reliable sources to help you discover and variously support your argument, and having cited these reliably, you may still have work to do to take full charge of your project, and to maintain your reader's good will and trust.

Whenever you use a source in a paper, you must determine, first, what *form* it should take to be most helpful and efficient (be that summary, paraphrase, mention, citation, or exact replication); second, whether you've made clear enough to your reader (however obvious it may be to you) exactly how your source bears on your argument; and third, whether you've also made clear to your reader when the source is speaking and when you are.

This chapter explains how to meet these responsibilities. It also describes the special techniques involved in directly quoting a source, and in thanking those who, though not technically sources, have provided you with relevant conversation, inspiration, or moral support.

2.1 Ways of Bringing a Source In

At any given point in your paper, a source will appear in one of a few basic forms. You will summarize or paraphrase its main ideas or findings, give its gist, or simply mention it in passing. Or you will reproduce parts of the source exactly, by replication or quotation.

(a) *Summary:* Here, you reduce a source text to its main point and aspects, using your own words but sometimes including quoted words or phrases from the source. When writing an essay about plagiarism in American universities, for example, you might summarize section 1.1 of this book as follows:

> ```
> The same source, Harvey notes, can play
> different roles in different situations,
> depending on a writer's purposes. He thus
> suggests that sources are best described
> by "what they are sources of" in a paper
> (data and ideas of different kinds) and
> what stance a writer takes toward them
> (accepting, rejecting, or qualifying).[1]
> ```

Note that this style of citation refers your reader to a footnote (see section 4.2) that gives the relevant pages in the source, this book. You will usually be summarizing longer texts than this—whole chapters, articles, or books—so the key requirement, that a summary be concise but accurate, will present a greater challenge. Two further requirements of summarizing are that you make clear whom or what you are summarizing (*Harvey notes*) and that you put your summary in your own words, except for phrases you place in quotation marks (or words in the source that have no real synonyms). This means that, to avoid plagiarizing, your summary must recast both the language *and* the sentence structure of the source.

(b) *Paraphrase:* Here, with the same requirements in force, your encapsulation follows more closely the source's particular order of presentation or reasoning:

> Sources, Harvey suggests, are best
> described by the role they play in partic-
> ular papers. This is a matter both of the
> kind of material that a source is offering
> and of what attitude or "stance" a writer
> takes toward it. While some sources tend
> to offer mainly factual material, includ-
> ing exact wording, statistics, testimony,
> and information, others provide ideas,
> including claims and concepts. Writer
> stances, he notes, tend to be accepting,
> rejecting, or qualifying (Harvey 3).

Note that this citation uses in-text, author-page style (see section 4.3). You should encapsulate by paraphrase, rather than summary, when the particular logic or order of a source's presentation is important to your argument. You will sometimes need to paraphrase not to encapsulate a long text, but to clarify a single pithy or difficult statement or concept. Such interpretive or explanatory paraphrasing, especially useful when writing about artistic or philosophical texts, will usually be longer than what it paraphrases. Unpacking the meaning of the short saying used later in this book, to take a trivial example, you might paraphrase thus:

> On this point Harvey invokes the prov-
> erb that "a stitch in time saves nine," by
> which he seems to mean that a step taken
> early to address a worsening situation
> will prevent the need for more difficult
> and elaborate action later on (48).

Your citation refers your reader to the page on which the saying is found, your sentence having made clear with the words *he seems to mean* that the paraphrase is your own.

(c) *Gist:* Here, you give only the main claim or thrust of a work or argument—in a sentence or so—without indicating many or any of its aspects or reasons. To give the gist of section 1.1 above, you might say that

> ```
> Harvey suggests that sources are best
> described by which one of a few basic
> roles they play in a given paper (2017).
> ```

Note that this citation and those in the following examples illustrate in-text author-year style (see section 4.4).

(d) *Mention:* Here, you refer to the source in passing, invoking it as part of a general characterization:

> ```
> Some analysts, such as Harvey, stress the
> roles that different sources play (2017).
> ```

(e) *Citation Only:* Here, you relegate the name of the source to a parenthetical citation or footnote:

> ```
> Still other analysts see the roles that
> sources play as the determining factor
> (Harvey, 2017).
> ```

[E] MENTIONING A TITLE IN YOUR PAPER

Italicize the title of a book (as in line 10 of Jennie's paper on p. 23) or collection, journal or newspaper, play, long poem, film, musical composition, or artwork. Put in quotation marks the title of an individual article, chapter, essay, story, or poem. Don't italicize the Bible or its books, or legal documents like the Constitution. For an italicized title that contains another title, indicate the latter by underlining (*The Making of <u>The Origin of Species</u>*) or by un-italicizing (*The Making of* The Origin of Species).

(f) ***Exact reproduction:*** Here, you replicate exactly an element of another source, such as a data table or a figure (e.g., a chart, graph, diagram, or map), or you quote exactly the words of the source, or, in an online paper, provide a link to the work in question (which you still must cite). Reasons to quote a source directly include the following:

- The source author has made a point so clearly and concisely that it can't be expressed any better.

- A certain phrase or sentence in the source is particularly vivid or striking, or especially typical or representative of some phenomenon you are discussing.

- An important passage is sufficiently difficult, dense, or rich that it requires you to analyze it closely, which in turn requires that the passage be produced so the reader can follow your analysis.

- A claim you are making is such that the doubting reader will want to hear exactly what the source said. This will often be the case when you criticize or disagree with a source; your reader wants to feel sure you aren't misrepresenting the source—or creating a straw man (or woman). In addition, you need to quote *enough* of the source so that the context and meaning are clear.

2.2 Three Basic Principles

Depending on the academic field, sources appear in some of the above forms more frequently than in others. Direct quotation, for example, is all but essential in literary papers, but is rare in the sciences and data-based social sciences. Three basic principles, however, should govern your thinking about how sources appear in any paper.

FIRST PRINCIPLE: *Use sources as concisely as possible, so your own thinking isn't crowded out by your presentation of other people's thinking and your own voice lost in your quoting of other voices.* This means that you should mention or summarize your source, perhaps quoting a vivid phrase or two, unless you have a good reason to paraphrase closely or quote more extensively.

SECOND PRINCIPLE: *Never leave your reader in doubt as to when you are speaking and when you are relying on material from a source.* Avoid ambiguity by (a) citing the source immediately after drawing on it, but also (if discussing the source or quoting it directly) by (b) announcing the source in your own sentence or phrases preceding its appearance and, for extensive quotation, by (c) following up its appearance with commentary about it or development from it that makes clear where your contribution starts, referring back to the source by name (*Compton's comment is questionable in several ways . . .*). Although you need not restate the name of your source where it's obvious, if your summary of it continues for many sentences you should remind your reader that you are still summarizing, not interpreting or developing.

You need not give the name or names of a source in advance when you merely mention it but don't quote it or discuss it at length (see the use of Bell, Schmidt, and Wills in the following excerpt). Be careful, however, that your citation doesn't come so late in your paragraph that it creates ambiguity about which ideas are yours and which are the source's.

THIRD PRINCIPLE: *Always make clear how each source you introduce into your paper relates to your argument.* This means indicating to your reader, in the words leading up to your summary, paraphrase, or quotation of a source, or in the sentences that follow and reflect on it (or both), what you want your reader to notice or focus on in the source and what your stance toward it is (see section 1.1 above and 2.3d below).

Notice how a student writer, Jennie, observes these three principles in this excerpt from a paper about why people engage in self-destructive behaviors like smoking and drinking:

1 Scientists distinguish between "proximate" and
2 "ultimate" explanations (Bell 600). An ultimate, long-
3 range explanation of smoking, based on a study of
4 human evolution, has greater appeal for many people
5 than a more localized, proximate explanation - like
6 chemical changes in the body or an oral fixation. But
7 ultimate explanations may conflict with proximate
8 evidence that seems more obvious, as does the
9 explanation proposed by physiologist Jared Diamond in
10 his recent book *The Third Chimpanzee*. Diamond cites
11 the theory of zoologist Amotz Zahavi that self-
12 endangering behaviors in animals (such as a male bird
13 displaying a big tail and a loud song to a female) may be
14 at once a signal and a proof of superior powers (196).
15 Such a bird has proved, writes Diamond, "that he must
16 be especially good at escaping predators, finding food,
17 resisting disease; the bigger the handicap, the more
18 rigorous the test he has passed." Humans share the
19 same instinct that makes birds give dangerous displays,
20 he suggests; and risky human actions, including the use
21 of drugs, are designed to impress potential mates and
22 competitors in the way Zahavi suggests risky animal
23 actions are (198). Diamond's characterization of the
24 message that teenagers send by smoking and drinking
25 creates an image of a strutting animal:

26   I'm strong and I'm superior. Even to take drugs
27   once or twice, I must be strong enough to get past
28   the burning, choking sensation of my first puff on
29   a cigarette, or to get past the misery of my first
30   hangover. To do it chronically and remain alive
31   and healthy, I must be superior. (199)

32 An apparent problem with this ultimate, evolutionary
33 explanation of smoking, however, is that people were
34 smoking long before they knew it was dangerous, before
35 they knew that doing it chronically made it harder to
36 "remain alive and healthy." Public concern about
37 smoking did not appear until the 1950s (Schmidt 29).
38 Before that, moreover, many people smoked in private —
39 removed from potential mates they might impress; men
40 had a quiet pipe by the fire or actually left the ladies (or
41 the ladies left them) to have a cigar after dinner. Finally,
42 Native American peoples smoked tobacco for centuries,
43 apparently for its pleasantly elevating effect (Wills 77).

In terms of the source roles mentioned in section 1.1, this excerpt breaks down as follows: Bell provides Jennie with a general concept (a distinction between types of explanation), which she accepts and applies to her own topic; Diamond provides her with a claim and an argument, which she rejects; and Schmidt and Wills provide her with information that she accepts as factual and as providing support for her claims that concern about smoking is recent and that Native Americans smoked tobacco for its pleasant effect. Later in the paper she uses, as sources of primary text, interviews she conducted with adolescents about their first smoking and drinking experiences.

In each case, Jennie uses her sources concisely and clearly. She summarizes, in passing, Bell's conceptual distinction. She reduces Diamond's 10-page argument about smoking and drinking to a few sentences and short quotations, and she merely refers her readers to Schmidt and Wills. She makes clear the relevance of the summary of Diamond to her argument in the sentence at lines 6–8 that leads up to the summary, providing an argumentative context for it (*But ultimate explanations may conflict with proximate evidence*) and then again by explicitly discussing the summarized material in the sentences following the quotation (*An apparent problem with this ultimate, evolutionary explanation*). Because her summary of Diamond continues for several lines, she reminds the reader at the beginning of line 20 (*he suggests*) that she is still summarizing. She also has been careful to paraphrase at those times in her summary when she may have been tempted merely to repeat her source's words. She paraphrases this sentence in Diamond's book:

> It seems to me that Zahavi's theory applies to many costly or dangerous human behaviors aimed at achieving status in general or at sexual benefits in particular.

And her paraphrase, at lines 20–23, differs from Diamond in both language and sentence structure:

```
risky human actions, including the use of
drugs, are designed to impress potential
mates and competitors in the way Zahavi
suggests risky animal actions are (198).
```

Jennie's paragraph also illustrates one further rule: *mention the nature or professional status of your source if it's distinctive.* Don't denote a source in a psychology paper as "psychologist Anne Smith" or in a literature paper as "literary critic Wayne Booth." But do mention professional qualification, especially where you are quoting, when it isn't apparent from the nature of the course or paper—as Jennie does, in this paper for an ethics course, when she uses a physiologist and a zoologist (lines 9–11). Additionally, do describe the nature of a source that is especially authoritative or distinctive—if it's the seminal article or standard biography, for example, or an especially famous or recent study, or by the leading expert or a firsthand witness.

[F] INDIRECT QUOTING AND CITING SUMMARIES

When you haven't actually read the original source, cite the passage as "quoted in" or "cited in" the source in which you found it—both to credit that scholar for finding the quoted passage or cited text, and to protect yourself in case he or she has misquoted, quoted out of context, or otherwise misrepresented. Also, *cite a summary account* of a text or a topic provided by another source, but use such an account only when that source is a scholarly one (see section 1.2); don't rely on a summary of an academic article or theory, for example, or of a historical phenomenon, that you find on the website of an advocacy group. And always read for yourself any source that's crucial to your argument, rather than relying on a summary.

2.3 Rules for Quoting

For both quotations that you embed in your own sentences and quotations that you quote as indented blocks, observe these general rules:

(a) *Quote only what you need or is really striking.* If you quote too much, you may convey the impression that you haven't digested the material or that you are merely padding the length of your paper. Whenever possible, keep your quotations short enough to embed gracefully in one of your own sentences. Don't quote lazily; where you are tempted to reproduce a long passage of several sentences, see if you can quote instead a few of its key phrases and link them with a concise summary.

(b) *Quote verbatim,* carefully double-checking the source after you write or type the words even if you have pasted in the quotation (texts can get jumbled in electronic transmission). Quote verbatim even if the source passage itself is misspelled or ungrammatical, indicating this by adding in brackets after the problematic word or phrase the italicized Latin word [*sic*], meaning "thus": Hemingway wrote that his editor "had a verry [*sic*] nice time at the bar." See Box H for the few minor exceptions to the rule of verbatim quotation.

(c) *Construct your own sentence so the quotation fits smoothly into it.* Jennie has done this at lines 15–18: *Such a bird has proved, writes Diamond, "that he must be especially good at escaping predators, finding food, resisting disease; the bigger the handicap, the more rigorous the test he has passed."* She has done this again, in a different way, at line 25, where she ends her announcing sentence with a colon and follows immediately with the quotation. (See Box G.)

(d) *Usually announce a quotation in the words preceding it* (as Jennie does in line 15 with *writes Diamond*) so your readers enter the quoted passage knowing who will be speaking and what they are listening for in the passage and won't have to reread the passage in light of this information. See 2.4a.

Withholding the identity of a quoted source until a citation at the end of the quotation is acceptable only when the identity of a quoted source is much less important than, or a distraction from, what the source says. This might be the case, for example, if you were giving a quick sampling of opinion—say, in a history paper, giving a series of short quotations illustrating a common belief in the divine right of kings, or in an English paper, quoting from a few representative early reviews of Walt Whitman.

(e) *Choose your announcing verb carefully.* Don't say "Diamond *states*," for example, unless you mean to imply a deliberate pronouncement, to be scrutinized like the wording of a statute or a biblical commandment. Choose rather a more neutral verb ("writes," "says," "observes," "suggests," "remarks," "argues") or a verb that catches exactly the attitude you want to convey ("laments," "protests," "charges," "replies," "admits," "claims," "objects"). Choose verbs carefully when summarizing and paraphrasing sources as well.

(f) *Don't automatically put a comma before a quotation,* as you do in writing dialogue. Do so only if the grammar of your sentence requires it (as Jennie's sentence at line 15, p. 23 does, whereas her sentence at line 36 does not).

(g) *Put the period or comma ending a sentence or clause after the parenthetical citation,* except after a block quotation (see section 2.4f).

(h) *Indicate clearly when you are quoting a passage* as you found it quoted in another source (see Box F).

[G] LINK QUOTATION AND
INTERPRETATION CONCISELY

1. The colon + quotation technique for announcing (see 2.3c) can also be used to avoid extra words when setting up or drawing out the significance of an embedded quotation. Instead of putting a quotation and its interpretation in separate sentences,

   Here the poet becomes self-mocking. He writes,
   "Oh, woe is me."

   or linking the two with a signal-word participle like "writing," "saying," or "exclaiming,"

   Here the poet becomes self-mocking, writing,
   "Oh, woe is me."

   you can sometimes more succinctly use the colon alone:

   Here the poet becomes self-mocking: "Oh, woe is me."

2. Quoted evidence can sometimes be neatly tucked inside an interpretive sentence, by means of parentheses, if the quotation is brief and its import clear. Instead of a choppy construction like this,

   The speaker knows that both paths are equally worn.
   He writes, "The passing there / Had worn them really
   about the same." He thus has chosen his future by
   whim.

   you may be able to insert the quotation in-between the interpretive elements:

   The speaker knows that both paths are equally worn
   ("The passing there / Had worn them really about
   the same") and thus that he has chosen his future
   by whim.

   The parenthetical technique is used in this text in the second sentence of section 2.4 below, p. 29.

2.4 Quoting Blocks

If you need to quote more than four lines of prose or two verses of poetry, indent the passage as a block. Jennie does this when she quotes three consecutive sentences of Diamond's book at line 26 (*"I'm strong and I'm superior"*) that give a particularly vivid statement of Diamond's theory. Doing this makes her paper more persuasive by giving her criticisms a specific focus, and it reassures readers that she is not misrepresenting Diamond by selecting a few weak or misleading phrases.

Quote a block only when you will consider closely the language of your source—for example, when discussing a speech by Lincoln, an argument by Kant, an eyewitness account of a revolution, or a key policy statement, but rarely in a science or social science paper—and only when you will follow up your quotation with some commentary on it. Otherwise, long passages of other people's voices will drown out your own voice and will take up space that you should be devoting to your own ideas. The basic rules for quoting blocks are as follows:

(a) *Tell your readers in advance who is about to speak and what to listen for.* Don't send them unguided through a long stretch of someone else's words. Notice how Jennie sets up the block quotation in lines 23–25, telling us beforehand both what we will be listening to and what we should listen for: *Diamond's characterization of the message that human teenagers send by smoking and drinking creates an image of a strutting animal.*

(b) *Usually construct your lead-in sentence so that it ends with a colon*—pointing the reader ahead (as Jennie does at line 25, on p. 23) to the quotation itself. Occasionally, clarity or momentum may be better served by having your lead-in sentence run directly into your quotation, in which case you may require a comma or no punctuation at all. But this should be the exception, not the rule.

(c) *Indent all lines 10 spaces (or 1")from the left margin,* to distinguish a block from a paragraph break. Single-space the block, to distinguish it further from the rest of the text, unless your instructor prefers double-spaced blocks (as do many publications for manuscript submissions).

(d) *Don't put an indented block in quotation marks;* the indenting replaces quotation marks. Use quotation marks in an indented block only where the source author is quoting or is reporting spoken words (as when Homer reports Achilles's funeral oration in the *Iliad*).

(e) *Follow up a block quotation with commentary that reflects on it and makes clear why you needed to quote it.* Your follow-up—unless you have discussed the quotation in the sentences leading up to it—should usually be a few sentences long, and it should generally involve repeating or echoing the language of the quotation itself, as you draw out its significance. Any quotation, like any fact, is only as good as what you make of it. After her block quotation of Diamond, Jennie follows up at length, echoing the language of the quotation (*"remain alive and healthy,"* line 36, p. 23) in her analysis of it. Another way to state this rule would be to *avoid ending a paragraph on a block quotation.* End with follow-up commentary that pulls your reader out of the quotation and back into your own argument about the quoted material.

(f) *When using an in-text, parenthetic system of citation, put your citation of a block quotation outside the period at the end of the last sentence quoted.* This makes clear that the citation applies to the whole block, not only to the last sentence quoted. Note that the citation (*199*) comes at the end of the block quotation in line 31 of Jennie's paper (p. 23).

[H] FITTING QUOTATIONS TO CONTEXT AND USING ELLIPSIS

There are a few cases in which you may need to adjust a quoted passage, in a very minor way, to fit its context in your paper.

(1) **To punctuate the end** of an embedded quotation, use whatever punctuation your sentence requires, not the source author's punctuation. In Jennie's sentence at lines 15–18, Diamond may or may not end his sentence after "passed"; however, since Jennie ends her own sentence there, she uses a period. *Put a period or comma inside the close-quotation mark,* as in lines 18 and 36 in the excerpt from Jennie; put colons and semicolons outside the close-quotation mark.

(2) **To emphasize** certain words in a quoted passage, in order to make them stand out, place in parentheses after your close-quotation mark the phrase (*my emphasis*) or (*emphasis added*). If the author has italicized the words, indicate this by adding (*Smith's emphasis*).

(3) **To add or change** a word in a quotation to make it fit into the grammar of your own sentence, which you should do only rarely, put brackets [ ] around the altered word. A source passage like "nostalgia for my salad days" might appear in your sentence as *he speaks of "nostalgia for [his] salad days."* A source passage like "I deeply distrust Freud's method of interpretation" might become *Smith writes that he "deeply distrust[s] Freud's method of interpretation."* Use this cumbersome device rarely; always try to construct your sentence so you can quote verbatim. If you need to change only an initial capital letter to a lowercase letter, do so silently, without putting brackets around the letter.

(4) **If the passage you quote contains a quotation,** use single rather than double quotation marks to indicate the source author's quoting.

(5) **To indicate a line break** in a quoted passage of poetry, use a slash (/), inserting a space before and after the slash: *Hamlet wonders if it is "nobler in the mind to suffer / The slings and arrows of outrageous fortune" or physically to act and thus escape them forever.*

(6) To omit words from the middle of a passage that you are quoting, *use ellipsis points*: three spaced periods inserted at the point of omission. *"Even to take drugs once or twice,"* Diamond writes, *"I must be strong enough to get past . . . the misery of my first hangover"* (199).

- If a sentence ends within the omitted portion, add an extra, fourth period and space, before the ellipsis, to indicate this.

- Don't use ellipsis marks at the start of a quotation, and only use them at the end if you are quoting a block and have omitted words from the end of the last sentence quoted.

- Don't omit only single words or short phrases, and never omit words in a way that gives a false sense of what the passage says (see section 3.3a).

- If the text you are quoting itself contains ellipsis marks, put the italicized word [*sic*] in square brackets immediately after the ellipsis.

2.5 Using Discursive Notes

Use a discursive footnote or endnote (also called a "substantive" or "content" note) when you want to make a comment, not just give publication details.

You may want to **tell your readers something extra** to the strict development of your argument. You may, for example, want to briefly amplify or explain something you have said, as does the note on page 12 of this book, and this note:

> 6. These differences are not small: in 1990 the US spent 45 percent more per capita than Canada, nearly three-quarters more than Germany and three times as much as the United Kingdom (Kingshorn 121; Connors 11).

Or direct readers to further items of interest, or acknowledge ideas of other scholars on the topic that resemble yours (see Box M) or that differ from them:

> 5. See chapter 3 of George Folsom's *Rectitudes* (London: Chatto, 1949) for an excellent summary of Gnostic doctrine and a slightly different critique of the ontological argument, stressing agency rather than effect.

Or notice, as an interesting aside, an implication or connection in your argument that your paper does not develop:

> 12. The use of the word "smelly" in this passage is illuminated by Jeffrey Myers's observation that Orwell "uses odor as a kind of ethical touchstone" (62). Orwell concludes his essay on Gandhi, Myers notes, by remarking "how clean a smell he has managed to leave behind" and says that the autobiography of Dali, the moral antithesis of Gandhi, "is a book that stinks."

Except in a long paper or thesis, however, use argument-related notes sparingly. In most cases, if the note is really interesting enough to include, you should work it into the argument of your paper (or save it for another paper).

You might also use a discursive note to **give extra information about sources**, for example about your use of a particular edition or of your own translation:

> 3. All translations from Pasteur are my own; I use the Malouf edition, which is based on an earlier and more complete draft of the treatise.

Or to say something about your citation system, or your use of terms or abbreviations:

> 2. Unless otherwise noted, references to Locke are to *Second Treatise of Government*, ed. C. B. Macpherson (Indianapolis: Hackett, 1980), which is cited by page number only.
>
> 3. Dickinson's poems are cited by their number in the Johnson edition, not by page number.
>
> 4. In this paper NK will refer to a natural cell-killer.

Where to put such discursive notes? If your paper cites sources by means of sequential footnotes or endnotes, include your discursive note in that sequence. If you're citing with reference to an alphabetical or coded list of references, create a separate section before the references list, but at the start of a new page, for sequentially numbered "Notes." If you have only one discursive note in such a paper, consider simply using an asterisk.

Finally, you may want to **acknowledge special help, influence, or support** from an uncited source, as discussed in Box C and illustrated by the following examples:

1. My understanding of Reconstruction is influenced by my reading of W. J. Cash's *Mind of the South* (New York: Knopf, 1941) and by stimulating discussions with Carol Peters and Tom Wah.

7. I am indebted for this observation and for the term "self-researching" to Susan Lin's comments in Anthro 25 class (2/6/16).

11. I wish to thank Roberto Perez for his objections to an earlier draft of this paper, and for directing me to the Gosson article.

1. Work for this assignment was done in collaboration with Vanessa Praz, who is mostly responsible for the "Methods" section.

6. I owe this example to Norma Knolls, whose help in understanding the mathematics of decision theory I gratefully acknowledge.

2. In this paper I use an analogy between soul and state developed in Prof. Caroline Hill's lectures for Sociology 144, Clark University, fall term 2013–14.

Science and social-science papers, which generally avoid discursive notes, often put acknowledgements of help in a special "Acknowledgements" section. In the humanities, if the help you're acknowledging is of a general kind, evident throughout the paper, put the raised reference number for your note after your title or at the point at which you first state your main idea. If it's help with a specific component, insert the note at the relevant point in the paper.

3

Misuse of Sources

Among other tests, in college you face the moral test of arriving at your own ideas and crediting those who have helped you, when it is sometimes tempting to do neither. This chapter concerns some failures to take charge, in your writing with sources, including large and small plagiarisms. These acts, whether arising out of laziness, panic, fatigue, despair, or misjudgment, involve a deception that undermines the trust on which the scholarly community depends; they will therefore land you in trouble in that community.

Moral exhortation has not been shown to prevent these misuses, perhaps because most students don't think themselves capable, beforehand, of such wrongdoing, and fall only unwittingly into misuse of sources. Given this, however, it can only help at least to know the different forms such wrongdoing can take, along with the situations in which it occurs and the habits and attitudes that make it more and less likely. Unsurprisingly, the different misuses of sources described here correlate with the different roles of sources defined in Chapter 1.

3.1 Plagiarism

In everyday conversation, the fact that some of our thoughts and phrases originate with others is treated casually. The fact is taken more seriously in scholarly conversation, where what may seem like name-dropping to outsiders is actually giving credit. In scholarly *writing*, when you are making a careful demonstration—the credibility of which depends on a careful distinguishing between what is yours and what is another's—the fact is taken very seriously indeed.

Plagiarism is the act of passing off the information, ideas, or words of another as your own, by failing to acknowledge their source—an act of lying, cheating, and stealing. *Plagiarus* means "kidnapper" in Latin; in antiquity, *plagiarii* were pirates who sometimes stole children. When you plagiarize, as several commentators have observed, you steal the brainchild of another.[1] Because you also claim that it's your own brainchild, however, and use it to get credit for work you haven't really done, you also lie and cheat. You lie to your instructor and other readers of your work, and you cheat both your source of fair recognition for his or her work and your fellow students who have completed the same assignment without plagiarizing.

In a recent study of more than 60,000 undergraduates, nearly 40% admitted to engaging in plagiarism at least once,[2] but incidents vary in seriousness and in circumstance. Many students have at some point in their careers obliviously or lazily incorporated a few phrases from a source, or simply absorbed a basic idea from a source that should probably have been cited. In such cases, the plagiarized material represents an insignificant contribution to the paper in question. When

---

1. See for example John Ciardi, *Good Words to You* (New York: Harper & Row, 1987), 225; and Lance Morrow, "Kidnapping the Brain Children," *Time*, December 3, 1990, 126.

2. Donald McCabe, "Cheating Among College and University Students: A North American Perspective," *International Journal for Educational Integrity*, no. 1 (2005): 1–11.

more substantial sections are involved, occasionally a student has been confused about the rules of acknowledgment. At the other end of the scale is the student who cold-bloodedly plagiarizes entire sections or a whole paper because he or she doesn't care about the course and is unwilling to put in the time.

Most often, however, the plagiarist knows the rules and has started out with good intentions but hasn't left enough time to do the work that the assignment requires. Perhaps the student had even downloaded sources from the Internet earlier, only to find later that the sources answer all of the interesting questions on the topic, or that he or she doesn't understand the material well enough to come up with the kind of paper that the assignment seems to want. The student has become desperate, is too embarrassed to get help or ask for another extension, and just wants the whole thing over with.

At this point, in one common scenario, the student gradually drifts over the moral line into plagiarism, getting careless while taking notes on a source or incorporating notes into a draft. The source's words and ideas blend and blur into those of the student, who at this point has neither the time nor the inclination to resist the blending and blurring. In another common scenario, the student panics and appropriates sections from one or more secondary sources or from another student's work—copying from the source directly and occasionally rephrasing a sentence, or closely paraphrasing the source without providing any citation—hoping to get away with it just this one time.

From the viewpoint of the school or college, the gradual line-crossing is no more acceptable than the sudden line-crossing. In both cases, the student is aware that what he or she is doing is wrong and chooses to continue rather than asking for more time or help, or accepting a lower grade for unoriginal but honestly cited work. The consequences of the discovered plagiarism are of course far worse than this (see Box I), and search engines and plagiarism checkers have made discovering it much easier.

[I] DISCIPLINARY CONSEQUENCES OF MISUSE

Minor violations are sometimes handled by the course instructor, who may fail the paper or require that the student rewrite it. For more serious cases, the student or students involved will receive a failing grade in the course; in addition, most institutions require instructors to forward such cases to a disciplinary committee for a hearing.

These committees, which may have student members, are typically thorough and fair. The accused is usually entitled to counsel and advice, has the right to write a statement and appear in person before the committee, and may appeal the decision. The lightest penalties for students found guilty involve a period of probation and a reeducation seminar, in addition to a failing grade in the course. More common is a period of suspension or even permanent expulsion.

This can be costly in the short run, in terms of lost tuition, and even more so in the long run: a disciplinary action that involves sources usually results in a permanent mark on the student's record. Most professional schools, graduate schools, and scholarships also require colleges to report any such infractions in their letters of recommendation, and require students to report them in their applications.

This is not to speak of the emotional cost—the process of being discovered or accused is harrowing, and not only a serious distraction from learning for the student but a cause of pain and embarrassment for the family.

3.2 Forms of Plagiarism

Plagiarism can occur in any kind of paper or presentation, from a short problem set or response paper to a long research paper or thesis. More common than wholesale copying, especially in longer papers, is piecemeal or "mosaic" plagiarism, in which a student mixes words or ideas of a source with his or her own words and ideas, *or* mixes uncited words and ideas from several sources into a pastiche, *or* mixes properly cited uses of a source with improperly or uncited uses. At any point in any paper, however, plagiarism usually takes one of the following forms:

(a) *Uncited data or information:* If you read p. 37 of this book for a paper you are writing on plagiarism in American colleges, and then you say in your paper that nearly 40% of undergraduates claim to have plagiarized, and you don't cite this booklet (p. 37), you are plagiarizing information that is not common knowledge. You need to cite such information, again, even when it isn't part of your main argument—when it appears in a "background" section of a paper or in accounts of previous work done on the topic. Your citation must accurately reflect your process: if you claim that you found the information about academic dishonesty in the 2005 journal article by McCabe itself (which you have not read), instead of as cited in *this* volume, you are misleading your reader and possibly embarrassing yourself (see Box F).

(b) *An uncited idea, whether a specific claim or a general concept:* Suppose you read the second paragraph of p. 37 of this book and then write this in your paper:

```
Many have attempted to give simple defini-
tions of plagiarism. Harvey, for example,
defines it as "passing off the information,
ideas, or words of another as your own, by
failing to acknowledge their source."³ But
plagiarism is not in fact a simple sin:
rather, it involves the dastardly trio
```

of lying, cheating, and stealing. Essen-
tially it means stealing the brainchild
- the idea - of another writer and claim-
ing it as your own, thereby gaining unfair
advantage over others who have done their
own work. "Plagiarism" is a particularly
appropriate word for the theft of brain-
children, since it comes from an ancient
Latin word for pirates who stole young
boys and girls.

_____

3. *Writing with Sources,* Third Edition
(Indianapolis: Hackett, 2017), 37.

Here you properly cite the quotation in the first sentence, and
the Latin etymology of child-stealer given in the last sentence
is common (dictionary) knowledge. But the idea of stealing
a *brain*child is not common, nor is the claim of the triple sin
involved in plagiarism. These distinctive ideas are plagiarized
from the final paragraph on p. 37 of this book, even though
you present them in a different order and in different words,
because they are uncited. Like the "But" that begins your second sentence, your citation in the first sentence of your paragraph is a deception. It makes readers think that you are fair
and scrupulous, and that you have a viewpoint distinct from
the source's, when in fact you are being both unscrupulous
and unoriginal.

(c) *An unquoted but verbatim phrase or passage:* Suppose
that you have read the second paragraph on p. 38 of this book
and you write this:

Plagiarism, as Harvey suggests, is often
the result of fatigue and panic. Imagine
that it is 3:00 A.M. The student in question, a good student and certainly not the
kind who would cold-bloodedly plagiarize a
whole paper, has started on his paper too
late. By the next afternoon, he has neither the time nor the inclination to fight
the blending and blurring of his sources'

```
words into his own. Imperceptibly, he
crosses a moral line.⁴
```

```
    4. Writing with Sources, Third Edition
(Indianapolis: Hackett, 2017), 38.
```

Here you end your paragraph with a citation that acknowledges a general reliance on the ideas of the source text, thus implying that all of the language is your own. Yet you have in fact borrowed several distinctive phrases verbatim, without quotation marks: "cold-bloodedly," "neither the time nor the inclination," "blending and blurring," "crosses a moral line." You may fix on certain words in a source as more striking than those around them, but this is all the more reason to give credit for the words by quoting, not simply citing. Beware of this kind of plagiarism, especially when you are summarizing background material that you don't think an "essential" part of the paper, or that you feel the source author has already summarized quite nicely.

(d) *An uncited structure or organizing strategy:* Look back over page 38. Suppose that, having read those paragraphs, you write this:

```
The occasions of plagiarism vary. Kim, a
foreign student, simply didn't understand
American notions of intellectual prop-
erty and citation. In his paper he relied
heavily on the idea of one book, to the
exclusion of his own ideas, thinking that
this was the best way to honor the writ-
er's authority. Michelle steeped herself
so thoroughly in her sources that, when
she wrote her paper, she took over a fun-
damental idea in them as a given and acci-
dentally reproduced some of their most
striking turns of phrase. Eric, having
taken invertebrate biology only because
it fit neatly into his schedule, did almost
none of the course reading and sim-
ply printed out a term paper he found on
```

the Internet. Glenn and Sara, more typical cases, actually liked the inverte-
brate course and intended to write good
papers for it, but simply ran out of time
to come up with their own ideas. Hur-
riedly bringing his paraphrased notes over
into his draft, just a few hours before
the deadline, Glenn started letting his
sources' ideas mix in with his own. About
this same time, Sara, who had been star-
ing at her blank computer screen all morn-
ing, was finally overwhelmed by anxiety and
went looking for the paper her roommate
had shown her that she had written for the
same class last year.

Your words and details here are indeed original, and the general idea that plagiarism occurs in different circumstances is obvious enough to count as common knowledge and doesn't need citing.

You have, however, taken the structural framework or outline of the passage directly from the source passage, which considers patch plagiarizing a result of (a) ignorance of the rules, or (b) oblivious absorption of an idea or replication of a phrase, in addition to (c) wholesale plagiarizing out of indifference or laziness, and (d) plagiarizing in a time panic, either by careless note-taking or deliberate copying. Providing no citation, you plagiarize a distinctive intellectual structure or way of proceeding with a topic—even though, again, your language differs from that of your source and your invented examples are original. You could have fairly introduced this latter fact and been credited for it by saying, for example, "The occasions of plagiarism (as mapped in a general way by Harvey) vary widely," and ending the sentence with a footnote.

[J] AVOID AMBIGUOUS OR INCOMPLETE CITING

Students who have cited incompletely in one of the following ways may find themselves accused of plagiarism.

- A source name is mentioned in the student's paper, at the point at which the source has been drawn upon, but no publication information has been provided in a citation or reference list.

- Author and publication information for the source is provided in a list of references but not cited at the point in the paper where the source is drawn upon.

- Author and publication information are given for a passage that draws heavily on a specific section of a source, but no page number is provided.

These are occasionally real oversights; but when readers are unable to find enough information to allow them to verify a source, they may suspect that the incomplete citing is attempting to disguise an over-reliance on a source—as it sometimes is. Students who then protest that the source *is* mentioned in the paper, and that they were simply sloppy about citing, face the difficult task of proving that their plagiarism was accidental.

3.3 Other Misuses of Sources

(a) *Misrepresenting Evidence:* When you have an idea or interpretation that you wish to be true—especially when the assignment is due shortly—you may be tempted to fudge your evidence to make it seem true. You may be tempted to ignore or sweep under the carpet evidence that you know doesn't fit, in which case you are simply betraying your own intelligence.

However, you may also be tempted into more serious violations of academic honesty. You might be temped to quote or paraphrase a source out of context or in misleading excerpts, so it seems to say what you want. You would be doing this if, in your essay on plagiarism in American colleges, you argued that most plagiarism in college papers is accidental, and you wrote the following:

```
Harvey believes that, although sometimes
a panicking paper-writer "has neither
the time nor the inclination" to resist
the incursion of a source's ideas, stu-
dents are "confused about the rules of
acknowledgment."5
```

> 5. *Writing with Sources*, Third Edition (Indianapolis: Hackett, 2017), 38.

The quoted passages can indeed be found on p. 38 of this volume, but the emphasis there—that only a *few* students are confused—is the opposite of what your summary implies.

Still more seriously, you might be tempted into altering or fabricating a source or some data. Because this kind of deception violates the basic principle of scholarly communities, in which members build on one another's work (the principle of valid reasoning based on true evidence), and because such a deception may suggest an inclination to commit similar acts in later life, it will usually result in serious action by the instructor or the school or college.

(b) *Improper Collaboration:* This occurs when two students submit more or less identical written work for an assignment on which they have worked together, and which is not a group presentation. Collaborative discussion and brainstorming is a vital activity for professional scholars; indeed, most articles in the sciences and social sciences have multiple authors. However, the author or authors of articles not only acknowledge in the completed article the contribution of other discussants, they also write the article on their own. When you are asked to collaborate on a project but are required to submit separate papers, you must write up your paper on your own, acknowledging the extent of your collaboration in a note (see section 2.5).

You and your partner(s) should not compose the report or exam or problem answers as you sit together or share a Google Doc, but rather write up notes. If you divide up the work (assuming the assignment allows it), don't write up your part and upload or send it to your partner, but rather send or bring notes to your meeting; and then *discuss* those notes, don't just copy them. Finally, beware of your partner's request, at the last minute and in a panic, to read over your finished report; you may be tempting him or her to plagiarize. Professional scholars do ask one another to read drafts; but again, in these cases only one paper is being produced, not two. If you're unsure about your instructor's policy on collaboration, ask.

(c) ***Dual or Overlapping Submission:*** Don't take it upon yourself to decide that work you plan to submit for one course, though in many places identical to work you will submit or have submitted for another course, is "different enough" by virtue of small changes you have made (e.g., an added section or an altered introduction or conclusion). When you are running late and need to submit a paper, don't simply submit a cut-and-pasted version of the paper you submitted for another course. Either act will land you in disciplinary trouble. You must first get permission from both instructors for such submissions. Be aware that, should your instructors give you permission for dual submission, they will likely require from you a longer paper than they require of other students in the course.

(d) ***Abetting Plagiarism:*** You are also guilty of misusing sources if you knowingly help another student plagiarize— whether by letting the student have or copy from your own paper, or by writing a paper or part of a paper for the student (as, for example, when in the course of "editing" a paper for another student, you go beyond correcting mechanical errors and begin rewriting significant portions of the paper). Any of

[K] AVOID ALL-BUT QUOTING

If your own sentences follow the source so closely in idea and sentence structure that the result is really closer to quotation than to paraphrase, you are plagiarizing, even if you have cited the source. You may not simply alter a few words of your source—even of a source such as an abstract you read for a literature review. You need to recast your summary into your own words and sentence structure (as in the example at the top of page 25), or quote directly.

these actions makes you liable to disciplinary action. It is right to be generous and collegial; however, when another student asks you for help with a paper, try whenever possible to phrase your comments as questions that will draw out the student's own ideas.

3.4 Bad Strategies and High-Risk Situations

Students who misuse sources usually don't plan to. They plan to write thoughtful papers that display their own thinking, but they get themselves into situations in which they either misuse sources from haste or negligence, or they come to believe that they have no choice *but* to misuse sources. Following are some (bad) ideas and attitudes that help create such predicaments.

1. "Start late; adrenalin will get you through." No, adrenalin may get you through an all-nighter; but for a substantial paper, starting a week before the due date may be starting late. You will always be surprised by how much thought and work a paper requires. This will be especially true for a paper that you have been putting off because you don't understand the material or simply haven't connected with the course. Procrastinating in such situations is a frequent cause of plagiarism.

2. *"Don't waste time writing until you know what you want to say."* No, in most cases, you won't know what you have to say until you do write—until you have jotted and assembled notes (the earlier you begin doing so, however casually, the better) and taken several cracks at formulating your main idea. To prevent a last-minute panic, set aside enough time to write a draft and a serious revision. If research is involved, set aside even more time to formulate a question, do research and become temporarily overwhelmed, reformulate your question in light of what your research revealed, then do more focused research. Arriving at an idea is the end of this process, not the start.

3. *"Just skim the assignment prompt, don't get bogged down in its details."* No, such skimming can in fact lead to late realizations and panic. Because even important aspects of an assignment may not be obvious immediately, read the prompt closely and revisit it while you are writing. The little time this takes is worth the plenty it can save: a stitch in time saves nine. Read the prompt when you first get it, jotting down initial thoughts or questions and get the topic turning over in your mind; this will allow you to notice relevant material in subsequent reading, lectures, and discussions. When you start taking notes and planning out the paper, read the prompt again to get clear on its goals, especially regarding how much, if any, research is required or permitted.

Read the prompt yet again when you start writing, at which point you're in a position to appreciate what the challenges of the assignment really are and what the prompt says about them. It may provide more definite advice and direction than you first realized, perhaps asking you to focus on a particular aspect of the topic, not to give the breezy overview of aspects you were planning; or to focus on a few primary sources, using secondary sources only for framing or not to use them at all.

4. *"Part of the assignment is guessing what your instructor expects."* No, although you do need to find your own way to write the paper, and no instructor likes to be asked to "just tell me what you want," it's the instructor's job to make clear the expectations of an assignment. Instructors, knowing the material and field so well, sometimes think these expectations are obvious when they aren't. If the assignment is confusing on a second read-through, when you've begun to plan and write, contact your instructor and go to his or her office hours. He or she may be able to provide or describe samples of this kind of paper from earlier classes, offer hypothetical theses or approaches, or suggest a good way to get started on the paper.

It's up to you to ask for clarification, however. The fact that an assignment doesn't fully explain itself does not excuse plagiarism.

5. *"Follow your interest above all."* Well, not above *all*. Discovering topics you care about is one of the skills of good writing. If, however, you decide to write on a topic which, although only tangential to the course or assignment, interests you so much that you're sure the paper will write itself, or about which you have discovered some irresistibly fascinating information, let your instructor know. If you light out on your own away from the assignment, especially if you do so late in the game, you may find yourself unexpectedly at a dead end or in an intellectual swamp. To work your way out, or to work out how your topic in fact does connect to the course, you may need to get an extension. Don't panic and try to solve your problem by plagiarizing.

6. *"To get the lay of the land, start every paper by doing an Internet search of key terms and skimming sources that turn up."* No; although this approach may indeed generate ideas, it's just as likely to overwhelm and paralyze you, alienating you from your own instincts and interests in the topic. Try instead to get down some of your own thoughts and responses early, so you have at least a starting point that is your own and that can help narrow your search. If the assignment itself doesn't ask prompting questions, try free-writing or brainstorming, formulating a hard question for yourself to answer,

locating areas of problem or conflict, imagining different viewpoints, or picking a few key passages and annotating them closely.

7. *"Do all your work on-screen, where the action is."* No, that can be the problem: too much action, not enough thought, since your computer is also where all the distractions are—not just e-mail and social media but thousands of further sources to check out. At a certain point, in working with sources online, you should change the scene and tempo by selecting and printing out the main sources you plan to use and sitting down elsewhere to read and annotate them. A significant challenge of writing with sources in the Internet age, the age of high volumes and high speeds, is simply to make yourself take time to digest and reflect upon your material with undistracted attention.

For the same reason, print out and take away to read the drafts of papers you write. Hard copy, especially if read aloud, makes it easier to notice problems in your expression and logic. It also makes it harder to ignore a questionable use of sources that may have seemed all right in the fluid online world.

8. *"When taking notes on sources, just summarize what they say; come up with your own ideas afterward."* No, in fact, this approach may leave you with a lot of summarized ideas and no time left to come up with your own. In general, take notes actively, not passively. Don't just copy down or summarize the source's words or ideas; record your reactions, reflections, questions, and hunches as you go. Note where you find yourself resisting, doubting, or puzzling over what a source says, or connecting it to something else; jot down possible arguments or observations you might want to make. These will provide starting points when you begin to frame the project of your paper, and they will help keep you from feeling overwhelmed by your sources—or your notes.

When you do summarize, don't loosely copy source material and simply change a few words; either summarize radically (see section 2.1) or quote exactly, using quotation marks.

[L] INTELLECTUAL PROPERTY
AND THE INTERNET

Working with sources online is no different, morally, than working with sources off shelves. Online sources may give the *impression* of not being anyone's intellectual property. The sheer volume of flowing information and ideas, their apparently merely virtual existence, the ease with which they can be appropriated and manipulated, the project of digitizing the world's libraries into a single pool of knowledge, the constant advances in storage and access technology that make conventions of attribution seem outdated, and attempts to update conventions seem tentative—all these factors contribute to that impression. So does the fact that much of the Internet in fact *is* unregulated, a network of sites freely importing, exporting, and adapting material from one another in spirit of open access, free borrowing, and common ownership.

But although human knowledge is indeed the inheritance of all humans, reliable knowledge is gathered, formulated, and established through the efforts of individuals, working in careful and regulated ways. The laissez-faire ethic of the web may be adequate for amateur assemblages of knowledge; but the scholarly enterprise, whereby painstaking work builds on earlier painstaking work toward truth, requires careful attribution.

9. "*Your paper is your responsibility; hole up and write it.*" Yes, writing does tend to be solitary work requiring you to ignore distractions; but even a little input from others can help greatly. Even if the assignment prompt doesn't require you to write in stages, for a paper of any length you should try to crystallize your early thoughts into a brief proposal or outline and get a brief response to this from your instructor or a classmate (who may want you to return the favor or even to exchange drafts for critique). Getting early feedback from others can help you get unstuck; it can give you ideas or tip you off to problems that, on your own, you may realize too late. And it gives you a living audience to imagine as you write, which can help you imagine what to say.

10. *"During your initial reading of sources, keeping track of publication information will only slow you down, and you may not even use some of the sources."* No. Here again, time taken early, to save publication data for all sources you read, will repay itself in the late stages of writing when time is short and when—because the book you need may be buried or back on the library shelf—you might be tempted to do the citation from memory or just to skip it altogether. Worse, if you have recorded source ideas anonymously, you may mistake them, willfully or not, for your own. URLs will remain in your browser's history, of course, but that history may get erased. If you cut and paste a passage from one place to another, you may forget where it came from, or the site may change or disappear; and, more dangerously, the passage may become detached from the source information. For these reasons, you should paste the URL to any source material you have copied. Also keep in mind that if questions arise about the source of your ideas, you may be asked to produce your notes, sources, and research process; so keep a copy of any key sections of online sources.

11. *"Compose your paper in the file where you have collected your sources and notes, so these can be readily drawn in."* No. In fact, they may be *too* readily drawn in, if you compose this way. The accidental or not-so-accidental blending of source ideas and language into paraphrase, and of paraphrase or summary into argument, is a major cause of plagiarism.

When you write with sources, work with at least two distinct files. Keep source material in one file, with publication information attached. Keep your notes on sources (your summaries and paraphrases, key quotations and commentaries), into which you copy only the most relevant excerpts from the sources themselves—in a separate file or at least in a different font or color (keep your source language in this font or color throughout the composing process). Compose your paper itself in a separate file, bringing in source material as needed for the argument you develop.

12. "Try to sound impressive and sophisticated, like a real scholar." No; although your style will show the influence of the scholars you read and the kinds of moves they make, don't *try* to sound more learned than you are. Your papers aren't expected to sound just like the articles you read, and indeed your intelligence will emerge most clearly in a plain, direct style. Such a style will also keep clear the distinction between your own thinking and your sources'. Once you begin to appropriate a voice that isn't yours, moreover, it becomes easier to appropriate words and ideas—to plagiarize. It's harder to be dishonest in a plain style than in a fancy one.

You may become paralyzed, especially in a field that's new to you, by an exaggerated idea of what would be an original enough idea for a paper. If this happens, get clarification from your instructor. When working with difficult sources, it can be an achievement simply to summarize plainly and accurately or to integrate your summaries. In such cases, you are usually not expected to resolve issues that experts have been debating for years, but only to organize the material and clarify the issues, bringing out their complexity, in your own way.

13. "Don't seek help if you find yourself in a jam; it's humiliating and will single you out to your instructor as a screwup." No! Plagiarizing can lead to a far greater humiliation and singling-out. Whatever has made you feel stuck, confused, or panicked about time—and there may be many reasons, including problems in your life—let your instructor know. He or she is spending less time thinking about your late paper than you imagine, and is more willing to help you succeed.

The sooner you make contact, the better. Make contact even if you feel embarrassed that you've let yourself get into the situation again, or because you haven't attended lectures or sections, or think you're the only student in the class who is having trouble (you aren't). If you feel that you have a special fear or block about writing papers, or procrastinate excessively, or if you have chronic difficulty organizing and prioritizing work, talk to a teacher or counselor.

14. *"In a pinch, borrow a friend's paper to inspire you, or borrow some notes to work with."* No, if you're really in a pinch, reading another student's finished paper may well discourage or panic rather than inspire you, and it may tempt you to plagiarize. Instead, ask the student to help you brainstorm some of your own ideas. As for borrowed notes, you have no way of knowing their source; they may come directly from a book or lecture, or from a book discussed in a lecture.

What you *should* do in a pinch, with all legitimate options exhausted, is face the music: hand in whatever you have written, cited honestly, and either ask apologetically for more time to complete the work and accept any grade penalty for this, or just accept the lower grade you may receive for too much mere summarizing. That grade will matter far less in the story of your life than will the consequences of plagiarizing.

[M] ENCOUNTERING "YOUR" IDEA IN A SOURCE

Should this happen, don't pretend that you never encountered the source—but don't panic either.

If it's your major idea and you're near the end of work on the paper, finish writing your argument as you have conceived it. Then look closely at the source in question; chances are that its idea isn't exactly the same as yours, that you have a slightly different emphasis or slant, or that you are considering somewhat different topics and evidence. In this case you can either mention and cite the source in the course of your argument (*"my contention, like Ann Harrison's, is that . . ."* or *"I share Ann Harrison's view that . . ."*), but stress the differences in your account—what you have noticed that Harrison hasn't. Go back and reshape your argument slightly, to bring out the different emphasis. If the argument in the source really is the same as yours, and you are in the midst of a long paper, go to your instructor, who may be able to suggest a slightly different direction for your paper. If you aren't writing a major paper, and/or haven't time to recast, use a note of acknowledgment:

> 12. In the final stages of writing
> this paper, I discovered Ann Harri-
> son's article "Echo and Her Medieval
> Sisters," *Centennial Review* 26.4
> (Fall 1982), 326-40, which comes to
> the same conclusion. See pp. 331-2.

Don't try to use such a note to cover plagiarism. Your instructor will know from your paper whether you had your own, well-developed idea before reading the source, and may ask you to produce your rough notes or drafts. (To be safe, always hold on to these until a paper has been returned.)

4

Styles of Citation

For reasons given at the end of Chapter 1, *that* you cite your sources is more important than *how* you do it. Knowing how, however, makes it easier to cite when you should. The mechanics of citing is an uninviting topic, but it's worth taking the time to learn the format of one or two methods. Not only is it instructive to understand, as you take courses in different fields, where and in what form scholars in a field expect to find sources cited; but making a habit of recording source information in a standard way will make you a more efficient writer, because you won't have to keep looking up formats when you're finalizing your work. Your consistency of practice will also reassure your reader.

This chapter describes the main methods of citing—the footnote, in-text, and coding methods. You may be asked to use the version of one of these methods that is found in a certain organization's publication manual, of which there are many. The chapter describes the styles of four of the most widely used manuals: the Chicago Manual (CMS), Modern Language Association (MLA), American Psychological Association (APA), and the Council of Scientific Editors (CSE). It gives the basic rules of each style and some commonly encountered special cases. Sample references in each style are found in the Appendix.

4.1 Documenting a Source: The Essentials

In any style of citing, your task is to give your readers enough information to locate and verify any item you use as a source. "Enough" information includes

- the author or authors (or organization, if no author is listed),
- the item title,
- the name of any volume that includes the item, and editor(s) if any,
- date of the item's or volume's publication (and revision, if any),
- the volume's (or site's) publisher or sponsor,
- page number(s) to which you refer, especially if you are quoting,
- for an online source, a locating URL or DOI.

When your source is an **article** in a journal, you give also its volume and issue number, and the article's inclusive page numbers. When your source is a **book** or report, you give also (except in MLA style) its place of publication.

For an online location, in many cases a stable URL will suffice. CSE formats require that it be preceded by the date you accessed the site: *[accessed yyyy-mm-dd]*; other styles ask for date of access only if the source has been revised since its original posting, or if an instructor or publisher requires it.

For citing scholarly articles, however, a permanent "digital object identifier" that locates an online document even if its Internet address changes, is now preferred. The DOI typically appears on the first page of an e-journal article or on the database homepage for the journal.

Because you can't supply all this source information in your text, you instead signal its availability nearby. Humanists typically signal by inserting a superscripted number at the end of a sentence that refers to a note at the foot or the page or end of the paper that contains the information (CMS); or they put in parentheses the author's last name and relevant page, which refer to an alphabetical list at the end of the paper that gives fuller details (MLA). Scientists and social scientists often either use the parenthetical method except inserting the year of publication after the author's name (APA and CSE); or they insert a superscripted symbol, a letter or a number, that refers to an item in a concluding list giving full information, but arranged in order of mention or other non-alphabetical order (CSE coding style).[1]

Details of these styles are given in this chapter and the Appendix following it, and on the websites of the organizations recommending the styles. The styles are also recognized by web-based citation programs that can automatically format the publication information you enter (see Box N). To use such programs, however, you need a basic understanding of how at least one signaling style works—and preferably more than one, because different courses may require you to use different styles.

[N] CITATION MANAGEMENT PROGRAMS

Software is now available that makes it a matter of a few keystrokes to record and store source information from searches, insert correct citations into a paper, and then create a properly formatted reference list— in whichever one of the many journal styles (including those described in sections 4.2–4.5) you choose. These programs create a personal database of materials on the web and can be accessed from anywhere (unlike resident citation programs, which store materials on your computer). They allow you to search databases as you work on your paper, and to store not only

---

1. Check for updates and other materials at www.hackettpublishing .com/wws3-support.

references but also notes you've taken on those references, keeping notes and references linked to but separate from sources themselves.

A citation management program is not, however, an automatic citation system. Software can't tell you when to cite, or whether to provide a page number, or even whether or not you should mention an author's name in your sentence—let alone whether that sentence properly distinguishes the author's ideas from your own. This remains your responsibility.

Note also that the advent of these programs means that there is less excuse than ever for losing reference information or allowing it to become detached from your sources, or for not linking reference information to a proper citation in your paper, or for letting your sources blur into your notes.

4.2 CMS Note Style

In this style, sometimes called "Chicago" style because it is recommended by the University of Chicago Press in its *Manual of Style* (CMS), you insert a raised reference numeral into your paper at the end of the sentence in which you draw on a source. This numeral refers your readers to a note at the bottom of the page (footnote) or end of the paper (endnote) that begins with the same numeral and gives information about the source:

> Diamond suggests that humans share the
> same "unconscious instinct" that makes
> birds give dangerous displays.[7]

Here, the raised 7 refers the reader to the following note—the first line of which is indented—that gives the source and page number:

> 7. Jared Diamond, *The Third Chimpanzee:
> The Evolution and Future of the Human Ani-
> mal* (New York: HarperCollins, 1992), 199.

Footnotes (or endnotes entitled "**Notes**") are used in books in all fields, and in papers in the humanities and some social sciences. They add minimal clutter to the body of your paper and disrupt the flow of your sentences less than do in-text citation styles.

Chicago format for an **online** reference (as shown in the Appendix and at www.hackettpublishing.com/wws3-support) requires you to provide a URL or DOI, and to provide the date of access only if the site changes often, or if required to by an instructor or publication.

> 27. Conrad J. Bladey, "The Potato
> Famine in History," http://www.intl.net
> /cksmith/famine/history.html.

CMS Basic Rules

Put your reference number whenever possible at the end of your sentence, outside the period and outside a close-quotation mark that follows the period:

> Diamond suggests that humans share the
> same "unconscious instinct" that makes
> birds give dangerous displays.[7]

> Diamond suggests that humans share the
> same "unconscious instinct."[1]

For clear attribution, however, you may occasionally need to put the reference number within your sentence (where it follows any punctuation except a dash, which it precedes), or to put one number within the sentence and another at the end:

> Although Jared Diamond suggests that
> humans share the same "unconscious
> instinct" that makes birds give danger-
> ous displays,[6] others have suggested a more
> political explanation for recklessness.[7]

To minimize the number of notes in a single passage, you may cite more than one source with a single reference number; however, you should always make clear which source pertains to which part of your sentence, using the "for/see" formula or a similar construction. You might cite Diamond and the "others" together at the end of the sentence in the previous example, and document them in a single note:

> 7. See Diamond's *The Third Chimpanzee: The Evolution and Future of the Human Animal* (New York: HarperCollins, 1992), 192–204. For a more psychological account, see Melvin Konner, *Why the Reckless Survive - and Other Secrets of Human Nature* (New York: Viking, 1990), esp. 133-37.

Citing a source for a second or subsequent time, you need only give the author's surname and a page reference:

> 8. Diamond, 196.

If you are using several sources by the same author, give an abbreviated title as well:

> 8. Diamond, *Third*, 196.

CMS Special Cases

(a) ***Submitting a bibliography at the end of your paper:*** When you are asked to do this, use the formatting given for *CMSbib* examples in the Appendix, and call the list "Bibliography," "Literature Cited," or "References."

(b) ***Referring to a specific passage in a literary work:*** Clarity may require you to give the location of the passage in your sentence (*at line 23 he writes* . . .). If not, give this location at the end of your note. For a **poem** of more than 12 lines, give the relevant line number or numbers. For a specific passage in a **novel** or long poem, give the chapter or section number before giving the page number (*Chap. 14, p. 26*). For a passage in a **play in verse**, instead of the page number give the act, scene, and line numbers, separated by periods:

> 6. *Hamlet*, ed. Harold Jenkins (London: Methuen, 1982), 3.1.56-68.

(c) *Reproducing an artwork or illustration:* Refer your readers to the figure or illustration number you have given it (*see figure 4*), and cite the source immediately below the item by artist, title, date, and source data:

> Illus. 4. Käthe Kollwitz, *Home Worker*, 1910 (charcoal 16″ x 22″, Los Angeles County Museum). In *Women Artists 1550-1950*, ed. Anne Sutherland Harris and Linda Nochlin (New York: Knopf, 1981), 264.

If you reproduce a table or figure (chart, graph, map, or other illustration) from a source, use the procedure described on p. 112. In a bibliography, if you have one, list artwork by the surname of the artist, and list a chart or graph by the source text's author.

4.3 MLA In-Text Style (Author-Page)

Scholars in some fields prefer that basic source information be available in the text of a paper itself. This information, placed in parentheses and referring to more complete documentation at the end of the paper, includes the author's or authors' last name(s), along with either the specific *page* on which the information, idea, or passage is found (in English studies and some other humanities fields) or the *year* in which the source was published (in the social sciences and sciences).

The parenthetical style developed by the MLA, an association of modern literature and language teachers, is an **author-page** style. Because author-page citing keeps the exact page location in the source attached to your use of the source passage in your paper, MLA style works well for papers about longer texts, and for literary or philosophical papers that quote and examine passages closely or include many different passages from the same source.

The author's name may appear in the sentence or in parentheses; the page number always appears in parentheses:

> Diamond has proposed that self-destructive human actions are an evolutionary signal of superior powers (196).

> A noted physiologist has proposed that self-destructive human actions are an evolutionary signal of superior powers (Diamond 196).

These signals in the sentence refer readers to an alphabetical list of "**Works Cited**," whose entries look like this:

> Diamond, Jared. *The Third Chimpanzee: The Evolution and Future of the Human Animal.* HarperCollins, 1992.

Note that MLA no longer requires that a book's place of publication be given. The MLA format for **online** sources in your "Works Cited" includes the date the item was published (and last updated, if applicable) and, after a period, a URL without protocol (no http:// or https://), or a DOI:

> Saletan, William. "Assembly Required: Constructing the First Artificial Life Form." *Slate*, 25 Jan. 2008. slate.com /id/2182573.

MLA formatting for many different kinds of sources is provided in the Appendix, and at www.hackettpublishing.com /wws3-support.

MLA Basic Rules

Whenever a source's particular formulation of ideas is important to your argument, give the author's name in your sentence:

> Jared Diamond proposes that self-destructive human actions are an evolutionary signal of superior powers (196).

```
As Diamond says, "the bigger the handicap,
the more rigorous the test he has passed"
(196).
```

Doing this also has the advantage of minimizing clutter at the end of your sentence. Note that the parenthetic citation goes *inside* the period that ends your sentence (except when quoting a block; see section 2.4f) and that, after a quotation, the citation goes outside the close-quotation mark, since it isn't part of the quotation. When you aren't discussing or quoting a source, you may put the name inside the parentheses with the page number:

```
Public concern about smoking appeared
much later (Schmidt 29).
```

When it's necessary to make clear that one part of your sentence comes from a source but another part from you (or another source), you may insert your reference mid-sentence. Put it at a natural pausing point, and inside the punctuation that ends the clause:

```
Although public concern about smok-
ing appeared much later (Schmidt 29), it
appeared precisely when the advertising
campaigns did.
```

MLA style assumes that a number following a name is a page number and not part of a name; do not put *p.* for "page" or *pp.* for "pages" or insert a comma between the name and the page number. If the idea or information you cite comes from two or more sources, however, use a semicolon to separate them in your citation (*Brill 103; Costa and Lerner 132*).

MLA Special Cases

(a) *Source in several volumes:* Give the volume number and a colon before the page reference, as in (*2: 347*) or (*Winslow 2: 347*).

(b) **Using more than one work by the same source:** Put an abbreviated title of the source in your citation, to indicate which of the texts you refer to—here, *The Third Chimpanzee:*

```
Jared Diamond proposes that self-destruc-
tive human actions are an evolutionary
signal of superior powers (Third 196).
```

(c) **Source with multiple authors:** For two or three authors, mention all of the names in the signal phrase in your sentence or put them in your parenthetic citation: (*Baker, Smythe, and Wills 207*). For more than three authors, use the first surname with *et al.* ("and others") in your sentence or in your citation: (*Belenky et al.*).

(d) **Source listing no author:** Use an abbreviated form of the title. An anonymous article called "Lost Tribes of the Gobi" might be cited as (*"Lost" 88*).

(e) **Quoting a source you found quoted by another scholar,** a source you know only from that quotation: Cite the source as "qtd. in" that scholar:

```
During the walk, according to Keats,
Coleridge "talked without stopping" (qtd.
in Murray 66).
```

(f) **Referring to a particular passage in a poem, novel, or play:** For a novel or poem, give the chapter or line number after the page number, following a semicolon:

```
In "Mending Wall," Frost at first does not
seem ironic when he says that "good fences
make good neighbors" (52; 1.27).
```

For a play in verse, cite the act, scene, and line numbers (separated by periods) instead of a page number:

```
When Hamlet says "O heart, lose not thy
nature," he means by "nature" his filial
feeling (3.3.351).
```

After a block quotation, however, put the citation outside the final period, since it applies to the whole block.

(g) *Reproducing an artwork or illustration:* Direct your readers to the figure or illustration number that you have given it (*see figure 5*). Beneath the item, or link to it, give the artist's full name, then the name of the work and its date. If your paper focuses on the artistic medium, include the medium of the work, its dimensions, and its location or owner:

```
John F. Kensett, Sunset with Cows, 1856.
Oil on canvas, 36 x 39 inches.
```

In your list of works cited, document the source from which you have taken the item, according to #34 or #35 in the Appendix. If you reproduce a chart, table, graph, or map, use the format illustrated on p. 112.

[O] CITING A REPEATEDLY DISCUSSED SOURCE: TWO TIPS

When you write a paper that closely analyzes, or refers repeatedly to, one or a few texts, you can use a discursive note to signal **an abbreviated form of citation.** You can do this in the following ways:

```
    1. Unless otherwise noted, ref-
erences to Locke are to The Second
Treatise of Government, ed. C. B.
Macpherson (Indianapolis: Hackett,
1980), which will be cited by page,
chapter, and section number.
    2. Act, scene, and line numbers
refer to Hamlet, ed. Harold Jenkins,
Arden edition (London: Methuen,
1982).
    3. Page references to NA refer
to Stevens's The Necessary Angel:
Essays on Reality and the Imagi-
nation (New York: Knopf, 1951); CP
```

is his *Collected Poems* (New York: Knopf, 1955), and OP his *Opus Post-humous*, ed. Samuel French Morse (New York: Knopf, 1957).

Such a note allows you to cite the source each time (by page, section, or line number, or abbreviation plus page, section, or line number) without having to footnote or supply author and date each time. Having provided the third note above, you might write later in your paper, *In one early poem, he sees the imagination is as a "bottle of indigo glass" (OP 22).*

When you refer to the **same source repeatedly in a paragraph** or passage, you need not repeat the citation at the end of every sentence but only when you refer to a different page in the source or start a new paragraph of your paper (as Jennie, on p. 23, doesn't give a new page reference for lines 15–18). Note, however, that your language needs to constantly make clear where you are drawing on a source—not giving your own ideas—by using phrasing like *"Aristotle further observes that. . . ."* It isn't enough, when your paragraph draws repeatedly on a source, simply to give a single citation at the start or end of that paragraph—unless you cast each sentence so as to preclude any ambiguity as to where the words, ideas, or information come from.

4.4 APA and CSE In-Text Styles (Author-Year)

Although citation styles in the social sciences and sciences tend to vary from publication to publication, most follow **author-year** style. In a psychology or biology paper, the year of publication matters more than the page number, because you are usually citing articles for their main idea or finding—not for a particular aspect or section, or for the wording of a particular passage (although a page number should be added for quoted or extensively paraphrased material). Moreover, you are often citing authors who have written many short papers on a subject, in a steady process of developing, testing, and correcting hypotheses, and your readers will want to know as they are reading whether you refer to later or earlier work.

In your paper, author-year style looks like this:

```
Recent explanations suggest that such
actions are evolutionary signals of supe-
rior powers (Diamond, 1992).
```

This is the author-year style for the social sciences that was developed by the American Psychological Association (APA). The author-year style recommended by the Council of Scientific Editors (CSE) is similar but in general slightly plainer. It does not insert a comma in the citation, for example, between author and year:

```
Recent explanations suggest that such
actions are evolutionary signals of supe-
rior powers (Diamond 1992).
```

Both styles include a page number after the date only when quoting a source directly (see p. 71). In both APA and CSE styles, the information in parentheses refers to an alphabetical list of "**References**," in which the date of publication is placed prominently, immediately after the author's name, which is emphasized by the indentation of all lines in a citation after the first. Following are examples of **APA** references:

Diamond, J. (1992). *The third chimpanzee:*
    The evolution and future of the human
    animal. New York, NY: HarperCollins.
Gottesman, C. (1999). Neurophysiological
    support of consciousness during waking
    and sleeping. *Progress in Neurobiology,*
    59, 469-508.

Note that these styles capitalize only the first significant word of a book or article's title and any proper nouns; and they do not place titles of articles in quotation marks. CSE is here again plainer, however. Whereas APA italicizes the titles of journals, magazines, and books, CSE does not; neither does it place a comma between the author's last name and initial, or place parentheses around the date of publication. Some examples of **CSE** references:

Diamond J. 1992. The third chimpanzee: the
    evolution and future of the human ani-
    mal. New York (NY): HarperCollins.
Gottesman C. 1999. Neurophysiological sup-
    port of consciousness during waking
    and sleeping. Progress in Neurobiology
    59:469-508.

For a book, if you refer only to a section, CSE recommends giving inclusive page numbers.

For **online** sources, APA and CSE formats again have minor differences. The publication date given in APA is that of initial creation or copyright or the most recent update:

Saletan, W. (2008, January 25). Assembly
    required: Constructing the first arti-
    ficial life form. *Slate.* Retrieved from
    http://www.slate.com/id/2182573

CSE includes a few more features:

Saletan W. 2008. Assembly required: con-
    structing the first artificial life form.
    Slate [magazine online]. [revised 2008
    Jan 25; accessed 2008 Jan 26].
    http://www.slate.com/id/2182573.

CSE format includes a date of revision (if any) and date of access in square brackets before the URL or DOI. Both manuals recommend using a DOI if possible (updates available at www.hackettpublishing.com/wws3-support).

APA/CSE Basic Rules

When you mention the author's name in your sentence, insert the year of publication immediately afterward, or at the end of the sentence, or at the end of the relevant clause—whichever makes clearer which are the source's thoughts and which are yours:

> Schmidt (1984) notes that public concern appeared much later.

> Schmidt notes that public concern appeared much later (1984), yet it appeared precisely when the major advertising campaigns did.

The parenthetical citation always comes inside the punctuation that ends your own sentence or clause.

When the idea or information cited comes from two or more sources, put the sources in alphabetical order, separated by a semicolon: in APA (*Schmidt, 1984; Tritt & Spank, 1985*) or in CSE (*Schmidt 1984; Tritt and Spank 1985*). If the two sources are by the same author, arrange them in chronological order, separated by a comma: in APA (*Schmidt, 1984, 1990*) or in CSE (*Schmidt 1984, 1990*).

When you repeatedly cite sources with multiple authors, whether you mention them in your sentence or cite them only in parentheses, observe these guidelines:

- If **two authors,** mention both names each time you cite: *Balough and Sterns (1988) found that* . . . , or in parentheses: APA (*Balough & Stearns, 1988*) or CSE (*Balough and Stearns 1988*).

- If **three to five authors,** the first time you mention or cite, use all the surnames: in sentence, *Belenky, Clinchy, Goldberger, and Tarule found that* . . . ; in parentheses, APA *(Belenky, Clinchy, Goldberger, & Tarule, 1986)* or CSE *(Belenky, Clinchy, Goldberger, and Tarule 1986)*. In subsequent mention or citation, give only the first surname followed by *et al.* In sentence: *Belenky et al. found that* . . . ; in parentheses (APA and CSE) *(Belenky et al., 1986)*.

- If **six or more authors,** mention or cite by the first author's surname and *et al.* from the start.

In both APA and CSE, **if you quote or refer to a specific passage,** or paraphrase a particular section of a book at length, include the page number(s) in your parenthetical citation. In APA, insert a *p.* for "page" or *pp.* for "pages":

```
As Diamond (1992) observes, "the bigger
the handicap, the more rigorous the test
he has passed" (p. 196).
```

```
Schmidt notes that public concern appeared
much later (1984, pp. 23-24).
```

APA/CSE Special Cases

(a) *Author is an organization with a long name:* Name it the first time in full, followed immediately by brackets containing the abbreviation that you will use in parentheses in all subsequent citations: (U. S. Department of Health and Human Services, 1989) [USDHHS].

(b) *No author listed:* Use a one- or two-word abbreviation of the title in your citation: *(Lost Tribes, 1990)*. For CSE style, omit the comma.

(c) *More than one source by the same author and year:* Cite and document the first source as *(Stearns & Wyn, 1990a)* and the second source as *(Stearns & Wyn, 1990b)*. For CSE style, omit the comma.

(d) *Reproducing an illustration, chart, or table:* In APA style, identify the item by placing above it a figure or table number, a title, and any required explanation. Put your citation below the item, starting with the word "Source" or "From," if you copy directly; "Redrawn from" if you redraw; and "Modified from" or "Adapted from" if you have made even minor changes. Then give the name, publication data, and page number, including the source again in your reference list:

> Figure 4. Performance by three groups of children on nine memory tasks. N = children of normal academic achievement; LD-N = learning-disabled children who performed in the average range on short-term memory tests; LD-S = learning-disabled children who performed poorly.

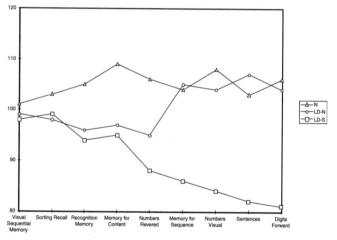

> *Source:* Farnham-Diggory, S. (1992). *The learning-disabled child.* Cambridge, MA: Harvard University Press, p. 121.

(e) *Personal communication:* Unless it can be retrieved or accessed by others, don't include in your reference list a personal interview you conducted, a letter or e-mail message you received, or a conversation you had. Give the information only in your text, as follows (in APA style):

```
A lawyer for the teachers, Diana Scholtz,
said that the action had been pending for
several years (personal communication,
April 1, 2007).
```

4.5 CSE Coding or Citation-Sequence Style

Some journals in the sciences require authors to identify each of their sources by a symbol or marker—usually a number but sometimes an initial letter of one or more author surnames. This number or letter appears in (parentheses) or [brackets] or as a superscript[E] in the paper each time that source is referred to, and it refers to a list of "References" at the end of the paper. Often, sources are coded by order of their first mention in the paper (by **citation sequence**). This sentence cites the third source mentioned in the paper:

```
Recent explanations have suggested that
such actions are evolutionary signals of
superior powers (3).
```

If this source is cited again, later in the paper, it is still identified by its code number (3), and it appears third in your list of references. In another version of the method, sources are coded by their number in an **alphabetic list** of references—in which case, the (3) in the example above would refer to the third source in the alphabetic list, rather than a citation-order list. Or, if you were coding **by initials**, Diamond might be cited at the end of the sentence as [D], and listed beside the symbol [D] in an alphabetical list of references. An article by Wallace, Dobbs, and Hershey might be coded as [WDH].

Like footnoting, coding has the advantage of requiring little apparatus in your text; like parenthetical citing, it eliminates the need to make a separate note each time you use a certain source—but it eliminates parenthetical information as well. Coding is appropriate for papers in the sciences, including biology, physics, chemistry, and math, where sources are mostly brief articles from which you don't directly quote, and in cases where you are not citing a great many sources (for which the coding system could become unwieldy).

If you aren't required to use the coding style of a particular publication, use this CSE version. To place citations in your paper, assign each source a number based on the order of first mention in your paper, and place the reference numbers in parentheses; or, if your instructor or publication prefers, use a raised numeral, as you would for a footnote. Both methods are illustrated below.

When you refer to several sources in the same citation, separate the numbers with commas (or superscripted commas), and arrange them in descending order of relevance or importance to your point:

```
Recent attempts to duplicated this result
have been unsuccessful.[7, 4]
```

If possible, place the numbers at the end of sentences, but place them earlier if necessary for clarity:

```
In accordance with published protocols
(12, 3, 8-10), purification of VP2 was
performed identically.
```

Follow the CSE rules for referring to multi-author sources, to graphics, and to personal communications, as described on pp. 70–73.

For your reference list, use the format for CSEcd shown in the Appendix. Note that this format differs from that of CSE in-text style. It places the first line of each entry, starting with the coding number, flush with the left margin and begins subsequent lines in the entry under the first letter of the name.

```
3. Diamond J. The third chimpanzee: the
   evolution and future of the human ani-
   mal. New York (NY): HarperCollins; 1992.
   325 p.
4. Gottesman C. Neurophysiological sup-
   port of consciousness during waking
   and sleeping. Prog Neurobiol. 1999;
   59:469-508.
```

Appendix
Listing Your References

This appendix illustrates the format for the source kinds listed, in the following styles: Chicago footnote or endnote (*CMSnt*), Chicago bibliography (*CMSbib*), Modern Language Association (*MLA*), American Psychological Association (*APA*), and the Council of Science Editors, both the style for alphabetic listing (*CSE*) and the style for a list coded by citation-sequence or another principle (*CSEcd*).

Start your list of references on a new page at the end of your paper, whether it be an MLA "Works Cited" list, an APA and CSE list of "References," or a CMS "Notes" list or "Bibliography," if you're writing a longer paper or thesis that requires one in addition to notes.

For footnotes, leave enough space at the bottom of each page to keep notes on the page to which they refer. Publications may prefer writers to double-space their notes and reference lists, but instructors often prefer that students single-space them, to set them apart visually from the body of the paper. Inquire about your instructor's preferences.

For cases that can't be extrapolated from these samples, check for further information, updates, and other materials at www.hackettpublishing.com/wws3-support.

Articles and Other Short Texts

Books and Longer Works

Oral, Visual, and Audio-Visual Sources

[P] SPECIAL SITUATIONS IN LISTING AUTHORS

- *Two authors:*

  Begin reference as follows:

CMSnt	Carla Williams and Robert O. Castle,
CMSbib	Williams, Carla, and Robert O. Castle.
MLA	Williams, Carla, and Robert O. Castle.
APA	Williams, C., & Castle, R. O.
CSE	Williams C, Castle RO.

- *Three authors:*

CMSnt	Henri Witt, Albert B. Lingren, and Willard Dobbs,
CMSbib	Witt, Henri, Albert B. Lingren, and Willard Dobbs.
MLA	Witt, Henri, et al.
APA	Witt, H., Lingren, B. H., & Dobbs, W.
CSE	Witt H, Lingren BH, Dobbs W.

- **Four or more authors:**

CMSnt	Kim-Sung Moon et al.
CMSbib	List all authors.
MLA	Moon, Kim-Sung, et al.
APA	List all authors, up to ten; for eleven or more, revert to first author + *et al.*
CSE	List all authors, up to ten, then add *et al.*

- **Repeated author:** List the entries by the same author, in APA and CSE styles, in chronological order, and repeat the author's name or names in second and subsequent entries. In CMS and MLA, list entries in alphabetic order of title, and use a triple dash instead of author name:

  > Geertz, Clifford. *The Interpretation of Cultures.* New York: Basic Books, 1973.
  >
  > ———. Works and Lives: *The Anthropologist as Author.* Stanford: Stanford UP, 1988.

- **Group or corporate author:** Use the group, organization, or corporation name instead of author name, e.g., American Historical Association, Minzano Inc., American Institute of Physics. If you abbreviate the group name in a paper using CSE style, begin the end reference with the acronym in brackets, followed by the full name:

  > [AIP] American Institute of Physics. 1990. Style manual. 4th ed. New York (NY): American Institute of Physics. 136 p.

In a CSEcd list, use the abbreviation only.

- *No author, editor, or organization given:* Start the citation with the title of the source. List the item according to the title's first word (not counting *a, an,* or *the*), following the style's general practice for handling titles.

- *Indirect Source:* For a source you cite parenthetically as "qtd. in" (MLA) or "as cited in" (APA) another scholar, list publication data for the other scholar. In CMS, give data for the original source *and* for the other scholar, linked by the phrase "quoted in" or "cited in":

> 1. Claude Levi-Strauss, *The Raw and the Cooked: An Introduction to a Science of Mythology* (New York: Harper & Row, 1969), 18, quoted in Howard Gardner, *Frames of Mind: The Theory of Multiple Intelligences* (New York: Basic Books, 1983), 103.

Articles and Other Short Texts

1. Article in a journal

CMSnt
> 1. Ann Harrison, "Echo and Her Medieval Sisters," *Centennial Review* 26, no. 4 (Fall 1982): 326-40.

CMSbib
> Harrison, Ann. "Echo and Her Medieval Sisters." *Centennial Review* 26, no. 4 (Fall 1982): 326-40.

MLA
> White, Hayden. "Foucault Decoded: Notes from the Underground." *History and Theory*, vol. 12, no. 1, Spring 1973, pp. 23-54.

APA　　Kahneman, D., & Tversky, A. (1979). Pros-
　　　　pect theory: An analysis of decision
　　　　under risk. *Econometrica*, *47*, 263-291.

CSE　　Farber E, Rubin H. 1991. Cellular adapta-
　　　　tion in the origin and development of
　　　　cancer. Cancer Res. 51: 275-276.

CSEcd　1.　Farber E, Rubin H. Cellular adaptation
　　　　in the origin and development of can-
　　　　cer. Cancer Res. 1991; 51: 275-276.

Give both issue and volume number, whenever available. APA style italicizes volume number, as part of the title. Abbreviate journal titles in CSE (see Box Q).

Citing only an abstract of the article: (a) When from the original source, insert *[Abstract]* after the title of the article; (b) when from a collection of abstracts, add to the end of the citation the name and volume of the collection of abstracts and the volume and page or the item number: *Abstract obtained from Psychological Abstracts, 67, Item 1121;* (c) when from a database, insert *Abstract from* after the citation, and follow the database formats already given. For an abstract of an unpublished talk, give the date of delivery before the database reference number.

[Q] ABBREVIATING PUBLICATION DATA

Don't include words like *Publishers, Co.,* and *Inc.* in your reference. In MLA style, abbreviate *University Press* to *UP.* Styles vary on abbreviating words such as *editor(s)* and *edited, translated, director,* etc., so check the examples. Abbreviate journal titles only in CSE style, except when the title is only one word. Follow the guidelines for abbreviation supplied by International Standard Serial Number website (www.issn.org).

2. *Article in a journal online (DOI)*

CMSnt   3. Nicholas Paskin, "Toward Unique
Identifiers," *Proceedings of the IEEE*
87, no. 7 (1999): 1208–1227, doi:
10.1109/5.771073.

CMSbib   Paskin, Nicholas. "Toward Unique Identifiers." *Proceedings of the IEEE*
87, no. 7 (1999): 1208–1227. doi:
10.1109/5.771073.

MLA   Paskin, Nicholas. "Toward Unique Identifiers." *Proceedings of the IEEE*, vol.
87, no. 7, 1999, pp. 1208–27. doi:
10.1109/5.771073.

APA   Paskin, N. (1999). Toward unique identifiers. *Proceedings of the IEEE*, *87*(7),
1208–1227. doi: 10.1109/5.771073

CSE   Paskin N. 1999. Toward unique identifiers. Proc IEEE. [accessed 2006 Mar 26];
87(7):1208–1227. doi:10.1109/5.771073.

CSEcd   5.   Paskin N. Toward unique identifiers.
Proc IEEE. 1999 [accessed 2006 Mar 26];
87(7):1208–1227. doi:10.1109/5.771073.

3. *Article in a journal online (URL)*

CMSnt   4. James Trier, "'Cool' Engagements
with YouTube: Part 2," *Journal of Adolescent & Adult Literacy* 50, no. 7 (2007):
598–603, http://onlinelibrary.wiley.com
/journal/10.1002/(ISSN)1936-2706.

CMSbib   Trier, James. "'Cool' engagements with You-
Tube: Part 2." *Journal of Adolescent &
Adult Literacy* 50, no. 7 (2007): 598–
603. *http://*onlinelibrary.wiley.com
/journal/10.1002/(ISSN)1936-2706.

MLA Trier, James. "'Cool' engagements with You-
   Tube: Part 2." *Journal of Adolescent &*
   Adult Literacy, vol. 50, no. 7, 2007,
   pp. 598-603. *Wiley Online Library*,
   onlinelibrary.wiley.com
   /journal/10.1002/(ISSN)1936-2706.

APA Trier, J. (2007). "Cool" engagements with
   YouTube: Part 2. *Journal of Adoles-*
   cent & Adult Literacy, *50*(7), 598-603.
   Retrieved from http://onlinelibrary
   .wiley.com/journal/10.1002/(ISSN)1936
   -2706

CSE Trier J. 2007. "Cool" engagements with
   YouTube: part 2. J Adol & Adult Lit.
   [accessed 2009 May 10];50(7):598-603.
   http://onlinelibrary.wiley.com
   /journal/10.1002/(ISSN)1936-2706.

CSEcd 6. Trier J. "Cool" engagements with You-
   Tube: part 2. J Adol & Adult Lit. 2007
   [accessed 2009 May 10]; 50(7):598-603.
   http://onlinelibrary.wiley.com
   /journal/10.1002/(ISSN)1936-2706.

4. Article in a magazine or newspaper

CMSnt 5. John Garamendi, "Clinton Offers a
   Managed Health-Care Plan," *New York Times*,
   October 8, 1992, late edition, A20.

CMSbib Garamendi, John. "Clinton Offers a Managed Health-Care Plan." *New York Times*,
   October 8, 1992. Late edition, A20.

MLA Walinksky, Adam. "The Crisis of Public
   Order." *Atlantic Monthly,* July 1995,
   pp. 39-54.

APA Shales, T. (1988, July 20). The Jackson
   triumph. *The Washington Post*, pp. C1,
   C6.

CSE   Margolis M. 1988 Aug 12. Thousands of
             Amazon acres burning. New York Times.
             Sect. B:1,8.

CSEcd   5. Margolis M. Thousands of Amazon acres
             burning. New York Times. 1988 Aug
             12;Sect. B:1,8.

Don't include a volume number for newspapers or magazines.
Note that APA puts "pp." before page numbers of a newspaper
article or anthology item, but not of a magazine or journal article.

5. Article in a magazine online

CMSnt   7. Jack Shafer, "Don't Call It Pla-
             giarism: Obama's Sound Bite, Considered,"
             Slate, February 25, 2008, http://www.slate
             .com/id/2184070.

CMSbib   Shafer, Jack. "Don't Call It Plagiarism:
             Obama's Sound Bite, Considered." *Slate*,
             February 25, 2008. http://www.slate
             .com/id/2184070.

MLA   Shafer, Jack. "Don't Call It Plagiarism:
             Obama's Sound Bite, Considered."
             Slate, 25, Feb. 2008, www.slate.com
             /id/2184070.

APA   Shafer, J. (2008, February 25). Don't call
             it plagiarism: Obama's sound bite,
             considered. *Slate*. Retrieved from
             http://www.slate.com/id/2184070

CSE   Shafer J. 2008 Feb 25. Don't call it
             plagiarism: Obama's sound bite,
             considered. Slate [magazine online].
             [accessed 2008 Mar 25]. http://www
             .slate.com/id/2184070.

CSEcd   3. Shafer J. Don't call it plagiarism:
             Obama's sound bite, considered.
             Slate [magazine online]. 2008 Feb 25
             [accessed 2008 Mar 25]. http://www
             .slate.com/id/2184070.

6. *Article in a newspaper online*

CMSnt   3. Karen Kaplan, "Flu Shots May Reduce Risk of Heart Attacks, Strokes and Even Death," *Los Angeles Times*, October 22, 2013, accessed February 11, 2014, http://articles.latimes.com/2013/oct/22/science /la-sci-sn-flu-shot-heart-attack-stroke -death-20131022.

CMSbib Kaplan, Karen. "Flu Shots May Reduce Risk of Heart Attacks, Strokes and Even Death." *Los Angeles Times*, October 22, 2013. Accessed February 11, 2014. http://articles.latimes.com/2013/oct/22 /science/la-sci-sn-flu-shot-heart -attack-stroke-death-20131022.

MLA   Kaplan, Karen. "Flu Shots May Reduce Risk of Heart Attacks, Strokes and Even Death." *Los Angeles Times*, 22 Oct. 2013, articles.latimes.com/2013/oct/22 /science/la-sci-sn-flu-shot-heart -attack-stroke-death-20131022.

APA   Kaplan, Karen. (2013, October 22). Flu shots may reduce risk of heart attacks, strokes and even death. *Los Angeles Times*. Retrieved from http://articles .latimes.com/2013/oct/22/science /la-sci-sn-flu-shot-heart-attack-stroke -death-20131022

CSE   Kaplan K. 2013 Oct 22. Flu shots may reduce risk of heart attacks, strokes and even death. Los Angeles Times. [accessed 2014 Feb 11]. http://articles.latimes .com/2013/oct/22/science/la-sci-sn-flu -shot-heart-attack-stroke-death -20131022.

CSEcd　　3.　Kaplan K. Flu shots may reduce risk of heart attacks, strokes and even death. Los Angeles Times. 2013 Oct 22; [accessed 2014 Feb 11 2014]. http://articles.latimes.com/2013/oct/22/science/la-sci-sn-flu-shot-heart-attack-stroke-death-20131022.

7. Letter to the editor

CMSnt　　1. Dorian Bowman, letter to the editor, *New York Times*, July 29, 2017, https://www.nytimes.com/2017/07/29/opinion/conservatives-and-health-care.html.

CMSbib　　Bernard, Cathy. Letter to the editor. *New York Times*, October 22, 2013. http://www.nytimes.com/2013/10/27/travel/letters-to-the-editor.html?r=0.

MLA　　Hamer, John. Letter. *American Journalism Review,* vol. 13, no. 3, Dec. 2006, p. 7.

APA　　Lott, J., Sr. (1997, September 4). [Letter to the editor]. *The Wall Street Journal*, p. A11.

CSE　　Smith KY. 2009. Dangers on the horizon [letter]. Am J Nucl Eng. [accessed 2010 May 2]; 12:15-16. doi:12.1109/6.771093.

CSEcd　　3.　Smith KY. Dangers on the horizon [letter]. Am J Nucl Eng. 2009;[accessed 2010 May 2]12:15-16. doi:12.1109/6.771093.

8. Article, section, or volume on a website

CMSnt　　27. John Fraser, "Nihilism, Modernism, and Value," Jottings.ca, n.p., January 21 2000, last modified May 9, accessed May 12, 2015. http://www.jottings.ca/john/peaks.html.

CMSbib   Fraser, John. "Nihilism, Modernism, and
          Value." Jottings.ca. January 21, 2000.
          Last modified May 9, Accessed May 12,
          2015. http://www.jottings.ca/john
          /peaks.html.

MLA   Linder, Douglas. "The Trial of Bill Hay-
          wood." *Famous American Trials*, Univer-
          sity of Missouri-Kansas City School of
          Law, 16 May 1999, law2.umkc.edu/faculty
          /projects/ftrials/haywood/haywood.htm.

APA   Jones, R. (2017, January 26). Corpse of
          weasel killed by large hadron collider
          displayed in twisted museum exhibition.
          Retrieved from http://gizmodo.com
          /corpse-of-weasel-killed-by-large
          -hadron-collider-displa-1791752513

CSE   Jones R. 2017 Jan 26. Corpse of weasel
          killed by large hadron collider
          displayed in twisted museum exhibi-
          tion. Gizmodo. [accessed 2017 Jan 27].
          http://gizmodo.com/corpse-of-weasel
          -killed-by-large-hadron-collider
          -displa-1791752513.

CSEcd   4. Jones R. Corpse of weasel killed by
          large hadron collider displayed in
          twisted museum exhibition. Gizmodo 2017
          Jan 26; [accessed 2017 Jan 27]. http://
          gizmodo.com/corpse-of-weasel-killed
          -by-large-hadron-collider-displa
          -1791752513.

For a website maintained by a private individual, such as the
independent scholar in the CMS examples, include the designation n.p. for "no publisher," and indicate date of access and of revision, if applicable. For a course-related, academic website (such
as the MLA example), the academic institution is the publisher.

9. Hosted comment on website item

Cite like a letter to the editor online, except using the provided username of the contributor as the author, and insert the phrase *Comment on* before the title of the item in question. Include also publisher, date, time, and URL.

MLA
Not Omniscient Enough. Comment on "Flight Attendant Tells Passenger to 'Shut Up' After Argument After Pasta." ABC News, 9 June 2016, 4:00 p.m., abcnews.go.com /US/flight-attendant-tells-passenger -shut-argument-pasta/story?id =39704050.

10. Story, poem, essay, or article in an edited anthology, collection, or proceedings

CMSnt
3. Richard Rodriguez, "The Achievement of Desire," in *The Essay: Old and New*, ed. Edward P. J. Corbett and Sheryl L. Finkle (Englewood Cliffs, NJ: Blair-Prentice Hall, 1993), 173.

CMSbib
Rodriguez, Richard. "The Achievement of Desire." In *The Essay: Old and New*, edited by Edward P. J. Corbett and Sheryl L. Finkle, 160-181. Englewood Cliffs, NJ: Blair-Prentice Hall, 1993.

MLA
Montrose, Louis. "Elizabeth Through the Looking Glass: Picturing the Queen's Two Bodies." *The Body of the Queen: Gender and Rule in the Courtly World, 1500-2000*, edited by Regina Schulte, Berghahn, 2006, pp. 61-87.

MLA   Goldsmith, Oliver. "The Deserted Village."
The Norton Anthology of English Litera-
ture, 5th ed., edited by M. H. Abrams
et al., Norton, 1986, pp. 2507-17.

APA   Salmond, A. (1974). Rituals of encounter
among the Maori: Sociolinguistic study
of a scene. In R. Bauman & J. Sherzer
(Eds.), *Explorations of the ethnography*
of speaking (pp. 192-212). New York,
NY: Cambridge University Press.

CSE   Hanawalt PC. 1987. On the role of DNA
damage and repair processes in aging:
evidence for and against. In: Warner
HR, editor. Modern biological theories
of aging. New York (NY): Raven Press.
p. 183-198.

CSEcd   5.   Cowan J. Resisting resistance. In:
Crepaldi G, Tiengo A, Del Prato S,
editors. Insulin resistance, metabolic
diseases, and diabetic complications.
Proceedings of the 7th European Sympo-
sium on Metabolism; 1998 Sep 30-Oct 3;
Padua, Italy. New York (NY): Elsevier;
1999. p. 27-47. (Excerpta Medica international congress series; 1117.)

List by item author, not the editor of the collection—unless you're
citing the whole volume, in which case cite by the name of the
editor or editors. For an item *from published conference* proceedings, include the inclusive page numbers of the item. For an item
excerpted in a class sourcebook, if you haven't consulted the
original place of publication, indicate your sourcebook's information title: e.g., *Sourcebook for Science B-35, Wetland Ecology, Prof.*
Jill Hurt. Colby College (Waterville, Maine), Fall Semester 2017. And
give inclusive page numbers for the original publication and in
the sourcebook.

11. Story, poem, essay, or article in a collection of an author's work

CMSnt   4. D. H. Lawrence, "Tickets, Please,"
             in *Collected Stories* (London: Heinemann,
             1974), 322.

CMSbib   Lawrence, David Herbert. "Tickets, Please."
             In *Collected Stories*. London: Heine-
             mann, 1974.

MLA   Hazlitt, William. "On Religious Hypocrisy."
             The Round Table. Dent, 1964, pp.
             131-38.

APA   Geertz, C. (1983). "Art as a cultural sys-
             tem." *Local knowledge: Further essays
             in interpretive anthropology* (pp.
             94-120). New York, NY: Basic-Harper.

CSE   Gould SJ. 1977. Ever since Darwin: reflec-
             tions on natural history. New York
             (NY): Norton. History of the vertebrate
             brain; p. 186-191.

CSEcd   4. Gould SJ. Ever since Darwin: reflections
             on natural history. New York (NY): Nor-
             ton; 1977. History of the vertebrate
             brain, p. 186-191.

12. Preface, foreword, introduction, or postscript to a book

CMSnt   8. Havelock Ellis, preface to *The
             Sexual Life of Savages,* by Bronislaw
             Malinowski (New York: Harcourt Brace,
             1929), vii.

CMSbib   Ellis, Havelock. Preface to *The Sexual Life
             of Savages,* by Bronislaw Malinowski,
             vii-xiii. New York: Harcourt Brace,
             1929.

MLA　　　Ellis, Havelock. Preface. *The Sexual Life of Savages*, by Bronislaw Malinowski, Harcourt Brace, 1929, pp. vii–xiii.

APA　　　Wills, R. (2010). Preface. In K. Wilson and J. Walker (Eds.), *Principles and techniques of biochemistry and molecular biology* (7th ed., pp. 1–6). New York, NY: Cambridge University Press.

CSE　　　Wills R. 2010. Preface. In: Wilson K, Walker J, editors. Principles and techniques of biochemistry and molecular biology. 7th ed. New York (NY): Cambridge University Press. p. 1–6.

CSEcd　　2.　Wills R. Preface. In: Wilson K, Walker J, editors. Principles and techniques of biochemistry and molecular biology. 7th ed. New York (NY): Cambridge University Press; 2010. p. 1–6.

13. Book review

CMSnt　　　7. Robert A. Huttenback, review of *Race and Empire in British Politics,* by Paul Rich, *American Historical Review* 93 (April 1988): 154.

CMSbib　　Huttenback, Robert. Review of *Race and Empire in British Politics,* by Paul Rich. *American Historical Review* 93 (April 1988): 153–55.

MLA　　　Leys, Simon. "Balzac's Genius and Other Paradoxes." Review of *Balzac: A Life,* by Graham Robb. *The New Republic*, 20 Dec. 1994, pp. 26–27.

APA　　　Geiger, J. (1987, November 8). [Review of the book *And the band played on,* by Randy Shilts]. *The New York Times Book Review,* 9.

APA   Kamp, David. (2006, April 23). Deconstructing dinner. [Review of the book *The
omnivore's dilemma: A natural history
of four meals*, by Michael Pollan.] *New
York Times*. Retrieved from http://www
.nytimes.com/2006/04/23/books/review
/23kamp.html

CSE   Kamp D. 2006, Apr 23. Deconstructing dinner. Review of: The omnivore's dilemma:
a natural history of four meals,
by Michael Pollan. New York Times.
[accessed 2009 May 1]. http://www
.nytimes.com/2006/04/23/books/review
/23kamp.html.

CSEcd   7.   Seals R. On the origin of origin
stories. Review of: A brief history
of creation: science and the search
for the origin of life, by B Mesler
and HJ Cleaves II. Am Scientist. 2016
[accessed 2016 Jan 14];104(3):184.
doi:10.1511/2016.120.184.

14. Article in an encyclopedia, Wikipedia, or other reference work

As shown, articles can be listed by subject, volume, author, or editor(s). S.v. means *sub verbo* ("under the word"), and n.d. means "no date," which applies to Wikipedia and other often-revised works. References to these may be inserted in your text with date of access ("Charivari," *Wikipedia* May 18, 2016) or listed as shown in the CSEcd sample.

CMSnt   3. Henry Dickinson Westlake, "Alcibiades," in *The Oxford Classical Dictionary*,
ed. Michael Cary et al. (Oxford: Clarendon,
1949), 31.

6. John Fleming, Hugh Honour, and Niko-
laus Pevsner, eds., *The Penguin Dictionary
of Architecture,* 2nd ed. (Harmondsworth,
UK: Penguin, 1972), s.v. "fillet."

7. *Encyclopaedia Britannica,* 11th ed.,
s.v. "Magna Carta."

CMSbib   Westlake, Henry Dickinson. "Alcibiades." In
The Oxford Classical Dictionary, edited
by Michael Cary et al. Oxford: Clarendon, 1949.

MLA   "Hannibal." *The Columbia Encyclopedia.* 6th
ed., Columbia UP, 2001.

Markie, Peter. "Rationalism vs. Empiri-
cism." *The Stanford Encyclopedia of
Philosophy,* edited by Edward N. Zalta,
Winter 2016, plato.stanford.edu
/entries/rationalism-empiricism/.

APA   Lichen. (2001). In *The Columbia encyclopedia* (6th ed.). New York, NY: Columbia
University Press.

McGhee, K., & McKay, G. (2007). Insects.
In *Encyclopedia of animals* (p.175).
Washington, DC: National Geographic
Society.

CSE   Westlake HD. 1949. Alcibiades. In: The
Oxford classical dictionary, Cary M et
al. editors. Oxford (England): Clarendon Press. p. 31.

CSEcd   3.   Westlake HD. Alcibiades. In: The Oxford
classical dictionary, Cary M et al.
editors. Oxford (England): Clarendon
Press; 1949. p. 31.

4.   "Charivari." *Wikipedia.* n.d.; [accessed
2016 May 18]. https://en.wikipedia.org
/wiki/Charivari.

15. Published interview

CMSnt 3. Candace Caldwell, "Lust of the Eye," interview by Malcolm Strong, *Visual Arts*, June 1995, 23.

CMSbib Caldwell, Candace. "Lust of the Eye." Interview by Malcolm Strong, *Visual Arts*, June 1995, 23-29.

MLA Caldwell, Candace. Interview with Malcolm Strong. "Lust of the Eye." *Visual Arts*, June 1995, pp. 23-29.

APA Strong, M. (1995, June). Lust of the eye. [Interview with Candace Caldwell]. *Visual Arts*, 23-29.

CSE Ross G. 2017. An Interview with Jerry Coyne. Am Sci. [accessed 2017 Jan 26]; 105(1). http://www.americanscientist .org/bookshelf/pub/an-interview-with -jerry-coyne.

CSEcd 5. Ross G. An Interview with Jerry Coyne. Am Sci. 2017; [accessed 2017 Jan 26]; 105(1). http://www.americanscientist .org/bookshelf/pub/an-interview-with -jerry-coyne.

16. Letter in a published collection

CMSnt 9. Virginia Woolf to Emma Vaughan, 12 August 1899, in *Congenial Spirits: Selected Letters of Virginia Woolf,* ed. Joan Trautman Banks (San Diego: Harcourt Brace, 1989), 5.

CMSbib Woolf, Virginia, to Emma Vaughan, 12 August 1899. In *Congenial Spirits: Selected Letters of Virginia Woolf,* edited by Joan Trautman Banks. San Diego: Harcourt Brace, 1989), 5-6.

MLA   Montagu, Lady Mary Wortley. "To Alexander Pope." 7 September 1718. *Selected Letters,* edited by Robert Halsband, Viking-Penguin, 1986.

APA   Montagu, Lady Mary Wortley. (1718, September 7). To Alexander Pope. In: *Selected Letters* (Robert Halsband, Ed.). New York, NY: Viking, 1986.

CSE   Montagu M. 1986. To Alexander Pope, 1718 Sept 7. In: R Halsband editor. Selected letters. New York (NY): Viking. p. 301.

CSEcd   3. Montagu M. To Alexander Pope, 1718 Sept 7. In: R Halsband editor. Selected letters. New York (NY): Viking; 1986. p. 301.

17. Letter or other papers from an archive

CMSnt   10. Ralph Young to David Simms, 11 May 1922, *Ralph Waldo Young Papers,* Harvard University Archives, Pusey Library, Cambridge, MA.

CMSbib   Young, Ralph. 11 May 1922, *Ralph Waldo Young Papers,* Harvard University Archives, Pusey Library. Cambridge, MA.

MLA   Campbell, David. "A Hobby." May 1944. Papers. Perkins Library, Duke University, Durham, NC.

APA   Axelrod, J. (1985). Memorandum on parks. The Julius Axelrod papers. 1915-1998. 22 boxes. Modern Manuscripts Collection, History of Medicine Division, National Library of Medicine, Bethesda, MD; MS C 494.

CSE   Stearns AA. 1864. Armory Square Hospital
           nursing diary. 70 leaves. Located at:
           History of Medicine Division, National
           Library of Medicine, Bethesda, MD; MS B
           372.

CSEcd   4. Axelrod J. Memorandum on parks. 1985.
           The Julius Axelrod papers. 1915–1998.
           22 boxes. Located at: Modern Manu-
           scripts Collection, History of Medicine
           Division, National Library of Medicine,
           Bethesda, MD; MS C 494.

18. Personal e-mail or letter

CMSnt   20. David Gewertz, letter to the
           author, September 8, 2006.

           21. Edgar Bowers, e-mail to the author,
           September 5, 1995.

MLA   Gewertz, David. Letter to the author. 8
           Sept. 2006.

           King, Marla. E-mail to the author. 16 Apr.
           2007.

Include in CMS as note only, not in bibliography. In APA and CSE, cite in your text only as (*D. Gewertz, personal communication, September 8, 2006*) for APA, or as (2006 *September 8*) for CSE. In all styles, cite such a communication as a source only if you are acknowledging a debt and/or if you can provide a copy of the text, should a reader request it.

19. Post to blog or archived discussion group

Use screen name as author name, if no other is provided.

CMSnt   6. Ella Morton, "Burning the Gävle
           Goat: Sweden's Holiday Tradition of Animal
           Arson" [blog], *Atlas Obscura*, December 16,
           2013, 11:05 a.m., accessed March 23, 2016,

　　　　　　http://www.slate.com/blogs/atlas_obscura
　　　　　　/2013/12/16/burning_the_g_vle_goat
　　　　　　_sSweden_s_unauthorized_holiday_tradition
　　　　　　_of_animal.html.

CMSbib　　Morton, Ella. "Burning the Gävle Goat:
　　　　　　　　Sweden's Holiday Tradition of Animal
　　　　　　　　Arson" [blog]. *Atlas Obscura*. December
　　　　　　　　16, 2013, 11:05 a.m., accessed March
　　　　　　　　23, 2016. http://www.slate.com/blogs
　　　　　　　　/atlas_obscura/2013/12/16/burning
　　　　　　　　_the_g_vle_goat_sSweden_s_unauthorized
　　　　　　　　_holiday_tradition_of_animal.html.

MLA　　　　Mann, Blain. "Equity and Equality Are
　　　　　　　　Not Equal" [blog]. *Education Trust*,
　　　　　　　　May 12, 2014, edtrust.org/the-equity
　　　　　　　　-line/equity-and-equality-are-not
　　　　　　　　-equal/.

APA　　　　Silver, N. (2013, July 15). Senate con-
　　　　　　　　trol in 2014 increasingly looks like
　　　　　　　　a tossup [Blog post]. Retrieved from:
　　　　　　　　http://fivethirtyeight.blogs.nytimes.com
　　　　　　　　/2013/07/15/senate-control-in-2014
　　　　　　　　-increasingly-looks-like-a-tossup

CSE　　　　Mann B. 2014 May 12. Equity and equality
　　　　　　　　are not equal [blog]. Education
　　　　　　　　Trust. [accessed 2017 Jan 28]. https://
　　　　　　　　edtrust.org/the-equity-line/equity
　　　　　　　　-and-equality-are-not-equal/.

CSEcd　　　3.　Mann B. Equity and equality are not
　　　　　　　　equal [blog]. Education Trust. 2014
　　　　　　　　May 12; [accessed 2017 Jan 28].
　　　　　　　　https://edtrust.org/the-equity-line
　　　　　　　　/equity-and-equality-are-not-equal/.

20. *Tweet*

In CMS use full name; in MLA, use screen handle; in APA, use name and screen handle. In all but CMS, include full tweet as title.

CMSnt   4. Justin Timberlake, Twitter post, June 16, 2014, 8:05 p.m. https://twitter .com/jtimberlake/status/478689830667186176.

CMSbib   Timberlake, Justin. Twitter post. June 16, 2014, 8:05 p.m. https://twitter.com /jtimberlake/status/478689830667186176.

MLA   @tombrokaw. "SC demonstrated why all the debates are the engines of this campaign." *Twitter*, 22 Jan. 2012, 3:06 a.m. twitter.com/tombrokaw/status/16099 6868971704320?lang=en

APA   Timberlake, J. [jtimberlake]. (2014, June 16). USA! USA!! Retrieved from https:// twitter.com/jtimberlake/status /478689830667186176

CSE   Timberlake J. 2014 Jun 16. USA! USA!! [accessed 2014 Jul 1]. https:// twitter.com/jtimberlake/status /478689830667186176.

CSEcd   6.   Timberlake J. USA! USA!! 2014 Jun 16; [accessed 2014 Jul 1]. https:// twitter.com/jtimberlake/status /478689830667186176.

Books and Longer Works

21. *Authored book*

CMSnt   1. Judith N. Shklar, *Ordinary Vices* (Cambridge, MA: Belknap-Harvard University Press, 1984), 39.

CMSbib   Shklar, Judith N. *Ordinary Vices*. Cambridge, MA: Belknap-Harvard University Press, 1984.

MLA   Trimpi, Wesley. *Ben Jonson's Poems: A Study of the Plain Style*. Stanford UP, 1962.

APA   Gardner, H. (1983). *Frames of mind: The theory of multiple intelligences*. New York, NY: Basic Books.

CSE   Woese CR. 1967. The genetic code: the molecular basis for genetic expression. New York (NY): Harper & Row. 486 p.

CSEcd   2. Woese CR. The genetic code: the molecular basis for genetic expression. New York (NY): Harper & Row; 1967. 486 p.

For an ***edition other than the first,*** indicate the designated edition immediately after title, with the phrase 2nd ed., 3rd ed., etc. (In APA, put this information in parentheses.) For a book ***published by a smaller branch or imprint of a large company*** (e.g., Belknap, of Harvard University Press; Anchor, of Doubleday), mention both, as in CMS example in #21.

22. *Edited collection, as a whole*

CMSnt   3. Nancy Peterson, ed., *Toni Morrison: Critical and Theoretical Approaches* (Baltimore: Johns Hopkins University Press, 1997).

CMSbib   Peterson, Nancy, ed. *Toni Morrison: Critical and Theoretical Approaches*. Baltimore: Johns Hopkins University Press, 1997.

MLA   Shulte, Regina, editor. *The Body of the Queen: Gender and Rule in the Courtly World, 1500-2000*. Berghahn, 2006.

APA   Duncan, G. J., & Brooks-Gunn, J. (Eds.). (1997). *Consequences of growing up poor*. New York, NY: Russell Sage Foundation.

CSE   Brogden KA, Guthmille JM, editors. 2002. Polymicrobial diseases. Washington (DC): ASM Press. [accessed 2014 Feb 28]. http://www.ncbi.nlm.nih.gov/books/NBK2475/.

CSEcd   3. Brogden KA, Guthmille JM, editors. Polymicrobial diseases. Washington (DC): ASM Press, 2002; [accessed 2014 Feb 28]. http://www.ncbi.nlm.nih.gov/books/NBK2475/.

23. Authored book with editor(s)

CMSnt   12. W. H. Auden, *Selected Poems,* ed. Edward Mendelson (New York: Vintage, 1979), 79.

CMSbib   Auden, W. H. *Selected Poems*. Edited by Edward Mendelson. New York: Vintage, 1979.

MLA   Forster, E. M. *Commonplace Book*. Edited by Philip Gardner, Stanford UP, 1985.

APA   Freud, S.(1971). *The psychopathology of everyday life* (J. Strachey, Ed.). New York, NY: Norton.

CSE   Da Vinci L. 1977. Literary works. Richter JP, editor. Commentary by C Pedretti. Berkeley (CA): University of California Press.

CSEcd   12. Da Vinci L. Literary works. Richter JP, editor. Commentary by C Pedretti. Berkeley (CA): University of California Press; 1977.

24. Electronic book

CMSnt   12. Lewis Carroll, *Alice's Adventures in Wonderland* (New York: Millennium, 1991), chap. 2, para. 6, http://quake.think.com /pub/etext/1991/alice-in-wonderland.txt.

        13. Rosalie-Garcia Rodriguez and Elizabeth White, *Self-Assessment in Managing for Results: Conducting Self-assessment for Development Practitioners*. World Bank Working Papers, 2005. doi:10.1596 /9780-82136148-1.

CMSbib   Carroll, Lewis. *Alice's Adventures in Wonderland*. New York: Millennium, 1991. http://quake.think.com/pub/etext /1991/alice-in-wonderland.txt.

MLA   Rodriguez-Garcia, Rosalie, and Elizabeth White. *Self-Assessment in Managing for Results: Conducting Self-Assessment for Development Practitioners*. World Bank Working Papers, 2005, doi:10.1596 /9780-82136148-1.

APA   Johnson, E. (1997, June 3). *No exits. Platforms of the future.* Retrieved September 20, 2006, from http://carol.cdma .books.com/6666/pof.htm

CSE   Brogden KA, Guthmille JM, editors. 2002.
           Polymicrobial diseases. Washington
           (DC): ASM Press. [accessed 2014 Feb
           28]. http://www.ncbi.nlm.nih.gov
           /books/NBK2475/.

CSEcd   3.   Brogden KA, Guthmille JM, editors.
                Polymicrobial diseases. Washington
                (DC): ASM Press; 2002 [accessed 2014
                Feb 28]. http://www.ncbi.nlm.nih.gov
                /books/NBK2475/.

25. Translated book

CMSnt   16. Friedrich Nietzsche, *The Gay
             Science*, trans. Walter Kaufmann (New York:
             Vintage, 1974), 86.

CMSbib   Nietzsche, Friedrich. *The Gay Science*.
           Translated by Walter Kaufmann. New
           York: Vintage, 1974.

MLA   Rousseau, Jean Jacques. "The Origin of
           Civil Society." *The Origin of Civil
           Society: Essays by Locke, Hume, and
           Rousseau*. Translated by Gerald Hopkins,
           edited by Sir Ernest Baker, Oxford UP,
           1947, pp. 212-68.

APA   Durkheim, E. (1957). *Suicide* (J. A. Spauld-
           ing & G. Simpson, Trans.). Glencoe, IL:
           Free Press.

CSE   Klarsfeld A, Revah F. 2003. The biology of
           death: origins of mortality. Brady L,
           translator. Ithaca (NY): Cornell
           University Press.

CSEcd   7.   Luzikov VN. Mitochondrial biogenesis
                and breakdown. Galkin AV, translator;
                Roodyn DB, editor. New York (NY):
                Consultants Bureau, 1985.

26. Reprinted book

A reprint is a reissue, often by a different publisher, not a new impression by the same publisher. The reference should provide at least the year of original publication, preferably also publisher and place.

CMSnt   14. Booker T. Washington, *Up From Slavery: An Autobiography* (1901; repr., New York: Doubleday Page, 1978), 34.

CMSbib   Washington, Brooker T. *Up From Slavery: An Autobiography*. 1901. Reprint, New York: Doubleday Page, 1978.

MLA   Wilder, Thornton. *The Bridge of San Luis Rey*. 1927. Washington Square, 1969.

APA   Allport, G. W. (1979). *The nature of prejudice*. Cambridge, MA: Addison-Wesley. (Original work published 1954)

CSE   Cranson R. 2006. Time in a bottle. New York (NY): Harper and Row. [Reprint of 1966]. 324 p.

CSEcd   5. Cranson R. Time in a bottle. New York (NY): Harper and Row; 2006. [Reprint of 1966]. 324 p.

27. Book in several volumes

CMSnt   13. Sandra Gilbert and Susan Gubar, *No Man's Land*, 2 vols. (New Haven, CT: Yale University Press, 1988), 1:90.

CMSbib   Gilbert, Sandra, and Susan Gubar. *No Man's Land*. 2 vols. New Haven, CT: Yale University Press, 1988.

MLA   Orwell, George. *Collected Essays, Journalism, and Letters*. Edited by Sonia Orwell and Ian Angus, Secker and Warburg, 1970. 4 vols.

Quintilian. *Institutio Oratoria*. Translated by H. E. Butler, vol. 2, Loeb-Harvard UP, 1980.

APA   Field, J. (Ed.). (1960). *Handbook of physiology* (Vol. 3). Washington, DC: American Physiological Society.

CSE   Alkire LG, editor. 2006. Periodical title abbreviations. 16th ed. Detroit (MI): Thompson Gale. 2 vol. Vol. 1, By abbreviation.

CSEcd   8. Alkire LG, editor. Periodical title abbreviations. 16th ed. Detroit (MI): Thompson Gale; 2006. 2 vol. Vol. 2, By title.

28. Book in a series

CMSnt   15. Carl Jung, "Anima and Animus," in *Aspects of the Feminine,* trans. R. F. C. Hull, Bollingen Series 20, vol. 27 (Princeton, NJ: Princeton University Press, 1982), 85-100.

CMSbib   Jung, Carl. "Anima and Animus." In *Aspects of the Feminine*. Translated by R. F. C. Hull. Bollingen Series 20, vol. 27. Princeton, NJ: Princeton University Press, 1982.

MLA   Peterson, Margaret. *Wallace Stevens and the Idealist Tradition*. UMI Research Press, 1983. Studies in Modern Literature 24.

APA   Tannen, D. (1989). Talking voices: Repetition, dialogue, and imagery in conversational discourse. In J. J. Gumpertz (Ed.), *Studies in interactional sociolinguistics* 6. Cambridge, England: Cambridge University Press.

CSE   Rosenthal LJ, editor. 2001. Mechanisms of
             DNA tumor virus transformation. New
             York (NY): Karger. 163 p. (Monographs
             in virology; vol. 23).

CSEcd   4. Rosenthal LJ, editor. Mechanisms of DNA
             tumor virus transformation. New York
             (NY): Karger; 2001. 163 p. (Monographs
             in virology; vol. 23).

If a **series editor** is listed, supply that name after the series name,
as in the APA example.

29. Dissertation

CMSnt   3. Susanna Ryan, "Coming to the Whip:
             Horsemanship and the Politics of Victorian
             Empathy" (dissertation, University of Mich-
             igan, 2002), 16–17.

CMSbib   Maschler, Yael Leah. "The Games Bilinguals
             Play: A Discourse Analysis of Hebrew-
             English Bilingual Conversation." PhD
             diss., University of Michigan, 1988.

MLA   Joyce, Joseph Patrick. *An Econometric
             Investigation of Government Preference
             Functions: The Case of Canada 1970–
             1980.* Dissertation Boston University,
             1984.

APA   Goffman, E. (1953). *Communication and con-
             duct in an island community* (Unpub-
             lished doctoral dissertation).
             University of Chicago, Chicago, IL.

CSE   Rush WF. 1972. The surface brightness of reflected nebulae [dissertation]. [Toledo (OH)]: University of Toledo.

         Neems D. 2016. The formation and function of lineage specific nuclear topologies during cellular differentiation [dissertation]. Evanston (IL): Northwestern University. 145 p.

CSEcd   3. Ryan S. Coming to the whip: horsemanship and the politics of Victorian empathy [dissertation]. [Ann Arbor (MI)]: University of Michigan; 2002. 202 p.

In CSE, brackets around place indicate an **unpublished** dissertation (Ryan), no brackets indicate a **published** dissertation (Neems), which is treated like a book, but includes before the publication data the designation diss., the university, and the year. Note that APA italicizes even an *un*published dissertation. If you are citing *only an abstract* of the dissertation, provide full information for the dissertation; then, after a period, give the name and volume of the collection of abstracts, the date, and the item number: *Dissertation Abstracts International,* 54 (1993): 1360B.

30. *Investigative or technical report*

CMSnt   8. Stanley Williams and Daniel Tibble, *Teaching with Technology,* ASCHE ERIC Higher Education Reports 3 (Washington, DC: George Washington University, 2001), 7.

CMSbib   Williams, Stanley, and Daniel Tibble. *Teaching with Technology.* ASCHE ERIC Higher Education Reports 3. Washington, DC: George Washington University, 2001.

MLA   Williams, Stanley, and Daniel Tibble. *Teaching with Technology.* ASCHE ERIC Higher Education Reports 3, George Washington University, 2001.

APA   Gorbunova, Y. (2013). *Laws of attrition:*
          Crackdown on Russia's civil society
          after Putin's return to the presidency.
          Human Rights Watch. Retrieved from
          http://www.hrw.org/sites/default/files
          /reports/russia0413_ForUpload_o.pdf

CSE   [APA] American Psychiatric Association.
          2000. Practice guidelines for the
          treatment of patients with eating dis-
          orders. 2nd ed. Washington, DC: Author.

CSEcd 8. Gorbunova Y. Laws of attrition: Crack-
          down on Russia's civil society after
          Putin's return to the presidency. Human
          Rights Watch; 2013 [accessed 2014 May
          7]. http://www.hrw.org/sites/default
          /files/reports/russia0413_ForUpload_o
          .pdf.

If *no author* is given, list by the sponsoring group or institution, as in the CSE example.

31. Government and other public documents

The great array of documents issued by the federal and other levels of government does not lend itself to a quick encapsulation of formats.[1] Following are some of the basic kinds of documents, along with the basic information needed to cite them:

- **Proceedings and debates of the House and Senate**, collected in the *Congressional Record* [include Congress # and session; *Cong. Rec.*, date, issue, page; subject or speaker, publication information]:

---

1. Federal documents are available online or in print from the Government Printing Office (GPO; http://www.gpo.org). For citation, *The Bluebook: A Uniform System of Citation*, published by the Harvard Law Review Association, is standard for many types of documents; and many university libraries have extensive websites devoted to citing these documents.

151 Cong. Rec. S1,630-31 (March 2, 2006)
    (statement of Sen. Leahy) http://www
    .gpoaccess.gov/index.html.

- **Court findings and arguments**, including those of the Supreme Court [include first plaintiff and defendant, volume name and page of the Law Report containing the case, name of deciding court, and year]:

Detroit Free Press, Inc. v. United States
    Department of Justice 829 F.3d 478 (6th
    Cir. 2016).

- **Enacted laws and amendments** (once a bill or resolution is passed) in the *Statutes at Large* for that year and later in the *U.S. Code* [include law title, Public Law#, passage date; title, volume, chapter, year, and pages in *Statutes* or *Code*]:

"Intermodal Surface Transportation Efficiency
    Act of 1991" (PL102240, Dec. 13, 1991).
    United States Statutes at Large, 105
    (1991) pp. 1914-2007.
Declaratory Judgment Act, U.S. Code, vol. 28,
    secs. 2101-2 (1952).
"Screening Passengers and Property," 49
    U.S.C. 44901, January 24, 2002, Available
    from: GPO Access, http://www.gpoaccess.gov
    /index.html.

- **Committee hearings** in the Senate and House [include legislative body, hearing title, Congress number, date or year; document number; publication information]:

U.S. House, Committee on Energy and Com-
    merce. Disapproving the FTC Funeral Rule,
    Hearing, May 4, 1983 (Serial No. 98-18).
    Washington: Government Printing Office,
    1983.
U.S. Congress, Senate, Committee on Environ-
    ment and Public Works, Global Climate
    Change: Hearings, 105th Cong., 1st sess.,
    1997, 202-205.

- **Reports by departments,** agencies, bureaus, and commissions [include legislative body, title, author (if identified), and publication information]:

  > Department of the Interior, Minerals Management Service, *An Oilspill Risk Analysis for the Central Gulf (April 1984) and Western Gulf of Mexico (July 1984)*, by Robert P. LaBelle. U.S. Geological Survey, Denver, 1983.

- **Regulations, advisories, and notices** of action on emergent situations falling under the *Code of Federal Regulations* [include section heading, title no., *CFR* section number, volume, number, date; publication information]:

  > "Dairy Product Price Support Program," Title 7 U.S. Code, Sec. 8771 et seq. 2006 ed. Supp. III, 2009. http://www.gpo.gov/index.html.

- **Executive orders and proclamations,** in the daily *Federal Register* [include title of item, kind of action and title number, date and pages; publication information]:

  > U.S. President, Proclamation, "National Alzheimer's Disease Awareness Month, 2013, Proclamation 9050," Federal Register 78, no. 214 (November 5, 2013): 66611, http://www.gpo.gov/fdsys/pkg/FR-2013-11-05/pdf/2013-26670.pdf.
  >
  > Executive Order 13228 of October 8, 2001, Establishing the Office of Homeland Security and the Homeland Security Council, Code of Federal Regulations, title 3 (2001): 796-802, http://www.gpo.gov/fdsys/pkg/CFR-2002-title3-vol1/pdf/CFR-2002-title3-vol1-eo13228.pdf.

Oral, Visual, and Audio-Visual Sources

32. Lecture, conference paper or poster, speech, or performance

Unless obvious, declare the genre after the title. If you access the source online, add the URL or DOI, as shown in the MLA and APA examples. Performances may also be listed by their playwright, composer, or individual artist, followed by their role (e.g., *cond., dir., chor.,* in CMS and APA; *conductor, director, choreographer* in MLA and CSE).

CMSnt
> 1. Rachel Adelman, " 'Such Stuff as Dreams Are Made On': God's Footstool in the Aramaic Targumim and Midrashic Tradition" (presentation, Annual Meeting of the Society of Biblical Literature, New Orleans, LA, November 21–24, 2009).

> 19. Helen Vaughan, "Robert Lowell" (lecture, Stanford University, Stanford, CA, November 12, 2003).

CMSbib
> Adelman, Rachel. " 'Such Stuff as Dreams Are Made On': God's Footstool in the Aramaic Targumim and Midrashic Tradition." Presentation at the Annual Meeting of the Society of Biblical Literature, New Orleans, LA, November 21–24, 2009.

MLA
> Prentiss, Mara. "Energy Revolution." Science Research Public Lectures. Harvard University Department of Physics, 23 Sept. 2015, Cambridge, MA. *YouTube*, uploaded by Harvard University. www.youtube.com/watch?v=RrA7KvTLDrc.

> *Othello*. By William Shakespeare. Directed by Jill Davies, performance by Newtown Players, Lyttle Theatre, Somerville, MA, 3 June 1993.

APA	Jacobson, T.E. & Mackey, T. (2013). What's in the name?: Information literacy, metaliteracy, or transliteracy [Power-Point slides]. Retrieved from http://www.slideshare.net/tmackey/acrl-2013
CSE	Antani S, Long LR, Thomas GR, Lee DJ. 2003. Anatomical shape representation in spine x-ray images. Paper presented at: VIIP 2003. Proceedings of the 3rd IASTED International Conference on Visualization, Imaging and Image Processing; Benalmadena, Spain.
CSEcd	7. Charles L, Gordner R. Analysis of MedlinePlus en Español customer service requests. Poster session presented at: Futuro magnifico! Celebrating our diversity. MLA '05: Medical Library Association Annual Meeting; San Antonio (TX); 2005.

33. Personal or telephone communication

In CMS style, include as note only, not in a bibliography.

CMSnt	20. Edgar Bowers, personal interview with the author, September 5, 1990.
MLA	Rice, Betina. Telephone interview. 6 Mar. 1993.
APA	Rolphe, C. (2014, July 29). Personal interview.

In CSE, and usually in APA (unless the material is especially significant to your paper) don't list an unpublished personal interview as a reference; instead, cite it in your paper as (*B. Rice, personal communication, 2003 March 6*). In all styles, cite such a source only if you are acknowledging a debt or if you can provide a copy of the text, should a reader request it.

34. Painting, photograph, or other artwork

If seen in reproduction, give also the information for the print or digital publication. If seen in-person only, in CMS give museum, exhibit, or owner information only in your text, parenthetically.

CMSnt   3. Käthe Kollwitz, *Home Worker*, 1925, Los Angeles County Museum, Los Angeles. In *Women Artists 1550-1950*, ed. Anne Sutherland Harris and Linda Nochlin (New York: Knopf, 1981), plate 107.

CMSbib   Kollwitz, Käthe. *Home Worker*, 1925, Los Angeles County Museum, Los Angeles. In *Women Artists 1550-1950*, plate 107, ed. Anne Sutherland Harris and Linda Nochlin. New York: Knopf, 1981.

MLA   Kollwitz, Käthe. *Home Worker*. 1925, Los Angeles County Museum, Los Angeles. *Women Artists 1550-1950*, edited by Anne Sutherland Harris and Linda Nochlin, Knopf, 1981, plate 107.

APA   Cartier-Bresson, H. (1938). *Juvisy*, France [photograph]. New York, NY: Museum of Modern Art.

Goya, Francisco. (1800). *The Family of Charles IV*. Museo Nacional del Prado, Madrid. *Museum syndicate*. Retrieved from http://www.museumsyndicate.com/item.php?item=2457

CSE   Goya F. 1800. The family of Charles IV. Museo Nacional del Prado, Madrid. Museum syndicate. [accessed 2010 May 30]. http://www.museumsyndicate.com/item.php?item=2457.

CSEcd   6. Kollwitz K. Home worker. In: Sutherland, HA, Nochlin L, editors. Women artists 1550-1950. New York (NY): Knopf; 1981. plate 107.

35. Image, graph, map, or table from a text or website

List a particular map, table, graph, chart, or plate by the title given in the text, followed (in MLA, APA, and CSE) by a word indicating the nature of the item and, if published in a book, its page and figure or plate number (if any). If the item is credited to an individual other than the book's author, list by that individual's name.

CMS
> 7. Wendy Otten, "Holland Canal," *Waterways* (New York: Sparshot, 1985), 12, fig 2.

CMSbib
> Otten, Wendy. "Holland Canal." In *Waterways*, 12, fig 2. New York: Sparshot, 1985.

MLA
> *Bear Habitat Before Columbus*. Map. Jennifer Tye. *The Way It Was*. Rollins, 1990, p. 34.

APA
> *Visual orientations* [Chart]. (1990). Madison: University of Wisconsin, Office for Health and Wellness. Figure 12.

CSE
> Office for Health and Wellness. 1990. Visual orientations [chart]. Madison: University of Wisconsin. Figure 12.

CSEcd
> 7. Field JK et al. Population smoking figures by index of multiple deprivation quintile [graph]. In: The UK lung cancer screening trial: a pilot randomised controlled trial of low-dose computed tomography screening for the early detection of lung cancer. Health Tech Assess; 2016 [accessed 2015 Jun 2]; 20(40). https://www.ncbi.nlm.nih.gov/books/NBK3627.

36. Film

If not citing by title (as in the CMS example), indicate the role of the person cited (e.g., director, producer, or both).

CMSnt   24. *Rashomon*, directed by Akira Kurosawa (1959; New York: Daiei, 1999). DVD.

CMSbib   *Rashomon*. DVD. Directed by Akira Kurosawa.
1959; New York: Daiei, 1999.

MLA   *In the Trenches*. Directed by Lionel Askins,
narrated by Albert Hamel, Cityfilm,
1992.

APA   Kurosawa, A. (Director). (1959). *Rashomon*
[Motion picture]. Tokyo: Daiei.

Stiller, B. (Producer) & Ayoade, R. (Director). (2011). *Submarine*. [Motion
picture]. United Kingdom: Film4
Productions.

CSE   How smart are animals? [video]. 2011 Feb 9.
NOVA scienceNOW. PBS. 53:06 minutes.
[accessed 2012 Mar 25]. http://video
.pbs.org/video/1777525840.

CSEcd   8. How smart are animals? [video]. NOVA
scienceNOW. PBS. 2011 Feb 9, 53:06
minutes; [accessed 2012 Mar 25].
http://video.pbs.org/video/1777525840.

37. Music recording or video

If accessed online, add URL, as shown in CMA and MLA examples.

CMSnt   23. Wolfgang Amadeus Mozart, *The Magic
Flute*, Vienna Philharmonic, conducted by
George Solti, Decca compact disc 3988.

CMSbib   Beyoncé, "Pray You Catch Me" in *Lemonade* (New York: Parkwood Entertainment, 2016). http://www.beyonce.com/album/lemonade-visual-album/.

MLA   Mozart, Wolfgang Amadeus. *The Magic Flute*. Conducted by George Solti, Decca CD 3988, 1970.

Beyoncé. "Pray You Catch Me." *Lemonade*, Parkwood Entertainment, 2016, www.beyonce.com/album/lemonade-visual-album/.

APA   Shocked, M. (1992). Over the waterfall. On *Arkansas traveler* [CD]. New York, NY: PolyGram.

Turner, A. (2013). Do I wanna know? [Recorded by Artic Monkeys]. On *AM* [MP3 file]. London, England: Domino Records.

CSE   Turner A. 2013. Do I wanna know? [Recorded by Artic Monkeys]. On: AM [MP3 file]. London, England: Domino Records.

CSEcd   4. Turner A. Do I wanna know? [Recorded by Artic Monkeys]. On: AM [MP3 file]. London, England: Domino Records; 2013.

38. Television or radio program

Indicate role of person or people cited, if not evident. If streamed from the Internet, add a URL as shown in the MLA and APA examples.

CMSnt   15. Juan Williams, "Aretha Franklin: A Life of Soul" [radio program], *NPR Online*, January 23, 2004, http://www.npr.org/templates/story/story.php?storyId=1472614.

CMS*bib* Williams, Juan. "Aretha Franklin: A Life of Soul" [radio program]. *NPR Online,* January 23, 2004. http://www.npr.org/templates/story/story.php?storyId=1472614.

MLA Garcia, Rodrigo, director. "All Happy Families." *The Sopranos.* 2004. *HBO,* www.hbo.com/sopranos/episode/season5/episode56.shtml.

APA Dick, L. (Writer), & Yaitanes, G. (Director). (2009). Simple explanation [Television series episode]. In P. Attanasio (Executive producer), *House, M.D.* Los Angeles, CA: Fox Broadcasting.

CSE Dick L, writer and Yaitanes G, director. 2009. Simple explanation [television series episode]. In: Attanasio P, producer, House, M.D. Los Angeles (CA): Fox Broadcasting.

CSEcd 6. Dick L, writer and Yaitanes G, director. Simple explanation [television series episode]. In: Attanasio P, producer, House, M.D. Los Angeles (CA): Fox Broadcasting; 2009.

39. YouTube video

If the author is not the uploader, include the author before the title and give the name of uploader (it may be an organization) after the title. Include as much descriptive information as necessary (including "YouTube") to make the nature of the material evident.

CMS*nt* 5. Jack Szostak, "The Origin of Cellular Life on Earth," Ibiology Seminars, January 11, 2012, http://www.youtube.com/watch?v=PqPGOhXoprU.

6. Jane McGonigal, "Gaming and Productivity," *YouTube*, uploaded by Big Think, July 3, 2012, http://www.youtube.com/watch?v=mkdzy9bWW3E.

CMSbib   McGonigal, Jane. "Gaming and Productivity." *YouTube*, uploaded by Big Think, July 3, 2012. http://www.youtube.com/watch?v=mkdzy9bWW3E.

MLA   Szostak, Jack. "The Origin of Cellular Life on Earth." Ibiology Seminars, 11 Jan. 2012. *Youtube*, www.youtube.com/watch?v=PqPGOhXoprU.

McGonigal, Jane. "Gaming and Productivity." *YouTube*, uploaded by Big Think, 3 July 2012, www.youtube.com/watch?v=mkdzy9bWW3E.

APA   Szostak, J. (2013, 11 January). The origin of cellular life on earth. *Ibiology Seminars*. Retrieved from http://www.youtube.com/watch?v=PqPGOhXoprU

McGonigal, J. (2012, 3 July). "Gaming and Productivity." *YouTube*, uploaded by Big Think. Retrieved from http://www.youtube.com/watch?v=mkdzy9bWW3E

CSE   Szostak J. 2013 Jan 11. The Origin of cellular life on earth, Ibiology Seminars. [accessed 2014 Jan 15]. http://www.youtube.com/watch?v=PqPGOhXoprU.

McGonigal, J. 2012 Jul 3. Gaming and productivity. YouTube, uploaded by Big Think. [accessed 2015 Jan 16]. www.youtube.com/watch?v=mkdzy9bWW3E.

CSEcd   5. Szostak J. The Origin of cellular life
             on Earth. Ibiology Seminars. 2013 Jan
             11; [accessed 2014 Jan 15]. http://www
             .youtube.com/watch?v=PqPGOhXoprU.

         6. McGonigal J. Gaming and productivity.
             YouTube, uploaded by Big Think 2012 Jul
             3; [accessed 2015 Jan 16]. www.youtube
             .com/watch?v=mkdzy9bWW3E.

40. Podcast

Indicate role of the person whose work you are citing, if someone
other than the author.

CMSnt   6. Malcolm Gladwell, "Generous Orthodoxy,"
            Revisionist History 9, podcast. November 7,
            2014, http://revisionisthistory.com
            /episodes/09-generous-orthodoxy.

CMSbib   Starecheski, Laura, producer. *Goat on a Cow*
             podcast. September 10, 2007. http://
             www.radiolab.org/story/91518-goat
             -on-a-cow/.

MLA   Starecheski, Laura, Producer. *Goat on a
             Cow* [Audio podcast]. 10 Sept. 2007,
             www.radiolab.org/story/91518-goat
             -on-a-cow/.

APA   Starecheski, L. (Producer). (2007, Septem-
             ber 10). *Goat on a Cow* [Audio podcast].
             Retrieved from http://www.radiolab.org
             /story/91518-goat-on-a-cow/

CSE   Starecheski L, producer. (2007, Septem-
             ber 10). Goat on a cow. Audio podcast.
             [accessed 2008 Aug 8]. http://www
             .radiolab.org/story/91518-goat-on-a
             -cow/.

CSEcd   7.   Starecheski L, producer. Goat on a cow.
Audio podcast. 2007 Sep 10; [accessed
2008 Aug 8]. http://www.radiolab.org
/story/91518-goat-on-a-cow/.